PREJUDICES

Prejudices

First Series

BY

H. L. Mencken

Ross & Perry, Inc.
Washington, D.C.

Ross & Perry, Inc. Publishers
216 G St., N.E.
Washington, D.C. 20002
Telephone (202) 675-8300
Facsimile (202) 675-8400
info@RossPerry.com

SAN 253-8555

Library of Congress Control Number: 2002105284
http://www.rossperry.com

ISBN 1-932080-14-7

Book Cover designed by Sapna. sapna@rossperry.com

☺ The paper used in this publication meets the requirements for permanence
established by the American National Standard for Information Sciences
"Permanence of Paper for Printed Library Materials" (ANSI Z39.48-1984).

CONTENTS

CONTENTS

PREJUDICES
FIRST SERIES

PREJUDICES: FIRST SERIES

I. CRITICISM OF CRITICISM
OF CRITICISM

EVERY now and then, a sense of the futility of
their daily endeavors falling suddenly upon
them, the critics of Christendom turn to a
somewhat sour and depressing consideration of the
nature and objects of their own craft. That is to say,
they turn to criticizing criticism. What is it in plain
words? What is its aim, exactly stated in legal
terms? How far can it go? What good can it do?
What is its normal effect upon the artist and the work
of art?

Such a spell of self-searching has been in progress
for several years past, and the critics of various
countries have contributed theories of more or less
lucidity and plausibility to the discussion. Their
views of their own art, it appears, are quite as divergent as their views of the arts they more commonly
deal with. One group argues, partly by direct statement and partly by attacking all other groups, that
the one defensible purpose of the critic is to encour-

age the virtuous and oppose the sinful—in brief, to police the fine arts and so hold them in tune with the moral order of the world. Another group, repudiating this constabulary function, argues hotly that the arts have nothing to do with morality whatsoever—that their concern is solely with pure beauty. A third group holds that the chief aspect of a work of art, particularly in the field of literature, is its aspect as psychological document—that if it doesn't help men to know themselves it is nothing. A fourth group reduces the thing to an exact science, and sets up standards that resemble algebraic formulæ—this is the group of metrists, of contrapuntists and of those who gabble of light-waves. And so, in order, follow groups five, six, seven, eight, nine, ten, each with its theory and its proofs.

Against the whole corps, moral and æsthetic, psychological and algebraic, stands Major J. E. Spingarn, U. S. A. Major Spingarn lately served formal notice upon me that he had abandoned the life of the academic grove for that of the armed array, and so I give him his military title, but at the time he wrote his "Creative Criticism" he was a professor in Columbia University, and I still find myself thinking of him, not as a soldier extraordinarily literate, but as a professor in rebellion. For his notions, whatever one may say in opposition to them, are at least magnificently unprofessorial—they fly violently in the

face of the principles that distinguish the largest and
most influential group of campus critics. As witness: "To say that poetry is moral or immoral is as
meaningless as to say that an equilateral triangle is
moral and an isosceles triangle immoral." Or,
worse: "It is only conceivable in a world in which
dinner-table conversation runs after this fashion:
'This cauliflower would be good if it had only been
prepared in accordance with international law.'"
One imagines, on hearing such atheism flying about,
the amazed indignation of Prof. Dr. William Lyon
Phelps, with his discovery that Joseph Conrad
preaches "the axiom of the moral law"; the "Hey,
what's that!" of Prof. Dr. W. C. Brownell, the Am-
herst Aristotle, with his eloquent plea for standards
as iron-clad as the Westminster Confession; the loud,
patriotic alarm of the gifted Prof. Dr. Stuart P. Sherman, of Iowa, with his maxim that Puritanism is the
official philosophy of America, and that all who dispute it are enemy aliens and should be deported.
Major Spingarn, in truth, here performs a treason
most horrible upon the reverend order he once
adorned, and having achieved it, he straightway performs another and then another. That is to say, he
tackles all the antagonistic groups of orthodox critics
seriatim, and knocks them about unanimously—first
the aforesaid agents of the sweet and pious; then the
advocates of unities, meters, all rigid formulæ; then

the experts in imaginary psychology; then the historical comparers, pigeonholers and makers of categories; finally, the professors of pure æsthetic.   One and all, they take their places upon his operating table, and one and all they are stripped and anatomized.

But what is the anarchistic ex-professor's own theory?—for a professor must have a theory, as a dog must have fleas.   In brief, what he offers is a doctrine borrowed from the Italian, Benedetto Croce, and by Croce filched from Goethe—a doctrine anything but new in the world, even in Goethe's time, but nevertheless long buried in forgetfulness—to wit, the doctrine that it is the critic's first and only duty, as Carlyle once put it, to find out "what the poet's aim really and truly was, how the task he had to do stood before his eye, and how far, with such materials as were afforded him, he has fulfilled it."   For poet, read artist, or, if literature is in question, substitute the Germanic word *Dichter*—that is, the artist in words, the creator of beautiful letters, whether in verse or in prose.   Ibsen always called himself a *Digter*, not a *Dramatiker* or *Skuespiller*.   So, I daresay, did Shakespeare. . . . Well, what is this generalized poet trying to do? asks Major Spingarn, and how has he done it?   That, and no more, is the critic's quest.   The morality of the work does not concern him.   It is not his business to determine whether it heeds Aristotle or flouts Aristotle.   He passes no judgment on its rhyme scheme, its length and breadth, its iambics, its politics, its patriotism, its piety, its psychological exactness, its good taste. He may note these things, but he may not protest about them—he may not complain if the thing criticized fails to fit into a pigeonhole. Every sonnet, every drama, every novel is *sui generis;* it must stand on its own bottom; it must be judged by its own inherent intentions. "Poets," says Major Spingarn, "do not really write epics, pastorals, lyrics, however much they may be deceived by these false abstractions; they express *themselves, and this expression is their only form.* There are not, therefore, only three or ten or a hundred literary kinds; there are as many kinds as there are individual poets." Nor is there any valid appeal *ad hominem.* The character and background of the poet are beside the mark; the poem itself is the thing. Oscar Wilde, weak and swine-like, yet wrote beautiful prose. To reject that prose on the ground that Wilde had filthy habits is as absurd as to reject "What Is Man?" on the ground that its theology is beyond the intelligence of the editor of the New York *Times.*

This Spingarn-Croce-Carlyle-Goethe theory, of course, throws a heavy burden upon the critic. It presupposes that he is a civilized and tolerant man, hospitable to all intelligible ideas and capable of reading them as he runs. This is a demand that at once rules out nine-tenths of the grown-up sophomores who carry on the business of criticism in America. Their trouble is simply that they lack the intellectual resilience necessary for taking in ideas, and particularly new ideas. The only way they can ingest one is by transforming it into the nearest related formula—usually a harsh and devastating operation. This fact accounts for their chronic inability to understand all that is most personal and original and hence most forceful and significant in the emerging literature of the country. They can get down what has been digested and redigested, and so brought into forms that they know, and carefully labeled by predecessors of their own sort—but they exhibit alarm immediately they come into the presence of the extraordinary. Here we have an explanation of Brownell's loud appeal for a tightening of standards—*i.e.*, a larger respect for precedents, patterns, rubber-stamps—and here we have an explanation of Phelps's inability to comprehend the colossal phenomenon of Dreiser, and of Boynton's childish nonsense about realism, and of Sherman's effort to apply the Espionage Act to the arts, and of More's querulous enmity to romanticism, and of all the fatuous pigeon-holing that passes for criticism in the more solemn literary periodicals.

As practiced by all such learned and diligent but essentially ignorant and unimaginative men, criticism is little more than a branch of homiletics. They judge

a work of art, not by its clarity and sincerity, not by
the force and charm of its ideas, not by the technical
virtuosity of the artist, not by his originality and
artistic courage, but simply and solely by his ortho-
doxy. If he is what is called a "right thinker," if he
devotes himself to advocating the transient platitudes
in a sonorous manner, then he is worthy of respect.
But if he lets fall the slightest hint that he is in doubt
about any of them, or, worse still, that he is indiffer-
ent, then he is a scoundrel, and hence, by their theory,
a bad artist. Such pious piffle is horribly familiar
among us. I do not exaggerate its terms. You will
find it running through the critical writings of practically all the dull fellows who combine criticism with
tutoring; in the words of many of them it is stated in
the plainest way and defended with much heat, theological and pedagogical. In its baldest form it shows
itself in the doctrine that it is scandalous for an artist
—say a dramatist or a novelist—to depict vice as attractive. The fact that vice, more often than not,
undoubtedly *is* attractive—else why should it ever
gobble any of us?—is disposed of with a lofty gesture. What of it? say these birchmen. The artist is
not a reporter, but a Great Teacher. It is not his
business to depict the world as it is, but as it ought to
be.

Against this notion American criticism makes but
feeble headway. We are, in fact, a nation of evan-

gelists; every third American devotes himself to im-
proving and lifting up his fellow-citizens, usually by
force; the messianic delusion is our national disease.
Thus the moral *Privatdozenten* have the crowd on
their side, and it is difficult to shake their authority;
even the vicious are still in favor of crying vice down.
"Here is a novel," says the artist. "Why didn't you
write a tract?" roars the professor—and down the
chute go novel and novelist. "This girl is pretty,"
says the painter. "But she has left off her under-
shirt," protests the head-master—and off goes the poor
dauber's head. At its mildest, this balderdash takes
the form of the late Hamilton Wright Mabie's "White
List of Books"; at its worst, it is comstockery, an idiotic and abominable thing. Genuine criticism is as
impossible to such inordinately narrow and cocksure
men as music is to a man who is tone-deaf. The
critic, to interpret his artist, even to understand his
artist, must be able to get into the mind of his artist;
he must feel and comprehend the vast pressure of the
creative passion; as Major Spingarn says, "æsthetic
judgment and artistic creation are instinct with the
same vital life." This is why all the best criticism
of the world has been written by men who have had
within them, not only the reflective and analytical
faculty of critics, but also the gusto of artists—
Goethe, Carlyle, Lessing, Schlegel, Saint-Beuve, and,
to drop a story or two, Hazlitt, Hermann Bahr, Georg

Brandes and James Huneker. Huneker, tackling "Also sprach Zarathustra," revealed its content in illuminating flashes. But tackled by Paul Elmer More, it became no more than a dull student's exercise, ill-naturedly corrected. . . .

So much for the theory of Major J. E. Spingarn, U. S. A., late professor of modern languages and literatures in Columbia University. Obviously, it is a far sounder and more stimulating theory than any of those cherished by the other professors. It demands that the critic be a man of intelligence, of toleration, of wide information, of genuine hospitality to ideas, whereas the others only demand that he have learning, and accept anything as learning that has been said before. But once he has stated his doctrine, the ingenious ex-professor, professor-like, immediately begins to corrupt it by claiming too much for it. Having laid and hatched, so to speak, his somewhat stale but still highly nourishing egg, he begins to argue fatuously that the resultant flamingo is the whole mustering of the critical *Aves*. But the fact is, of course, that criticism, as humanly practiced, must needs fall a good deal short of this intuitive recreation of beauty, and what is more, it must go a good deal further. For one thing, it must be interpretation in terms that are not only exact but are also comprehensible to the reader, else it will leave the original mystery as dark as before—and once interpre-

tation comes in, paraphrase and transliteration come
in. What is recondite must be made plainer; the
transcendental, to some extent at least, must be done
into common modes of thinking. Well, what are
morality, trochaics, hexameters, movements, historical
principles, psychological maxims, the dramatic unities—what are all these save common modes of thinking, short cuts, rubber stamps, words of one syllable?
Moreover, beauty as we know it in this world is by
no means the apparition *in vacuo* that Dr. Spingarn
seems to see. It has its social, its political, even its
moral implications. The finale of Beethoven's C
minor symphony is not only colossal as music; it is
also colossal as revolt; it says something against
something. Yet more, the springs of beauty are not
within itself alone, nor even in genius alone, but
often in things without. Brahms wrote his Deutsches
Requiem, not only because he was a great artist, but
also because he was a good German. And in
Nietzsche there are times when the divine afflatus
takes a back seat, and the *spirochaetae* have the floor.

Major Spingarn himself seems to harbor some
sense of this limitation on his doctrine. He gives
warning that "the poet's intention must be judged at
the moment of the creative act"—which opens the
door enough for many an ancient to creep in. But
limited or not, he at least clears off a lot of moldy
rubbish, and gets further toward the truth than any

of his former colleagues. They waste themselves
upon theories that only conceal the poet's achievement the more, the more diligently they are applied;
he, at all events, grounds himself upon the sound notion that there should be free speech in art, and no
protective tariffs, and no *a priori* assumptions, and
no testing of ideas by mere words. The safe ground
probably lies between the contestants, but nearer
Spingarn. The critic who really illuminates starts
off much as he starts off, but with a due regard for
the prejudices and imbecilities of the world. I think
the best feasible practice is to be found in certain
chapters of Huneker, a critic of vastly more solid influence and of infinitely more value to the arts than
all the prating pedagogues since Rufus Griswold.
Here, as in the case of Poe, a sensitive and intelligent
artist recreates the work of other artists, but there
also comes to the ceremony a man of the world, and
the things he has to say are apposite and instructive
too. To denounce moralizing out of hand is to pro-
nounce a moral judgment. To dispute the categories
is to set up a new anti-categorical category. And to
admire the work of Shakespeare is to be interested in
his handling of blank verse, his social aspirations,
his shot-gun marriage and his frequent concessions
to the bombastic frenzy of his actors, and to have some
curiosity about Mr. W. H. The really competent
critic must be an empiricist. He must conduct his ex-

ploration with whatever means lie within the bounds of his personal limitation. He must produce his effects with whatever tools will work. If pills fail, he gets out his saw. If the saw won't cut, he seizes a club. . . .

Perhaps, after all, the chief burden that lies upon Major Spingarn's theory is to be found in its label. The word "creative" is a bit too flamboyant; it says what he wants to say, but it probably says a good deal more. In this emergency, I propose getting rid of the misleading label by pasting another over it. That is, I propose the substitution of "catalytic" for "creative," despite the fact that "catalytic" is an unfamiliar word, and suggests the dog-Latin of the seminaries. I borrow it from chemistry, and its meaning is really quite simple. A catalyzer, in chemistry, is a substance that helps two other substances to react. For example, consider the case of ordinary cane sugar and water. Dissolve the sugar in the water and nothing happens. But add a few drops of acid and the sugar changes into glucose and fructose. Meanwhile, the acid itself is absolutely unchanged. All it does is to stir up the reaction between the water and the sugar. The process is called catalysis. The acid is a catalyzer.

Well, this is almost exactly the function of a genuine critic of the arts. It is his business to provoke the reaction between the work of art and the spectator.

The spectator, untutored, stands unmoved; he sees the work of art, but it fails to make any intelligible impression on him; if he were spontaneously sensitive to it, there would be no need for criticism. But now comes the critic with his catalysis. He makes the work of art live for the spectator; he makes the spectator live for the work of art. Out of the process comes understanding, appreciation, intelligent enjoyment—and that is precisely what the artist tried to produce.

II. THE LATE MR. WELLS

THE man as artist, I fear, is extinct—not by some sudden and romantic catastrophe, like his own Richard Remington, but after a process of gradual and obscure decay. In his day he was easily the most brilliant, if not always the most profound, of contemporary English novelists. There were in him all of the requisites for the business and most of them very abundantly. He had a lively and charming imagination, he wrote with the utmost fluency and address, he had humor and eloquence, he had a sharp eye for the odd and intriguing in human character, and, most of all, he was full of feeling and could transmit it to the reader. That high day of his lasted, say, from 1908 to 1912. It began with "Tono-Bungay" and ended amid the last scenes of "Marriage," as the well-made play of Scribe gave up the ghost in the last act of "A Doll's House." There, in "Marriage," were the first faint signs of something wrong. Invention succumbed to theories that somehow failed to hang together, and the story, after vast heavings, incontinently went to pieces. One had begun with an acute and highly diverting study of monogamy in modern London; one found one's self, toward the close, gaping over an unconvincing fable of marriage in the Stone Age. Coming directly after so vivid a personage as Remington, Dr. Richard Godwin Trafford simply refused to go down. And his Marjorie, following his example, stuck in the gullet of the imagination. One ceased to believe in them when they set out for Labrador, and after that it was impossible to revive interest in them. The more they were explained and vivisected and drenched with theories, the more unreal they became.

Since then the decline of Wells has been as steady as his rise was rapid. Call the roll of his books, and you will discern a progressive and unmistakable falling off. Into "The Passionate Friends" there crept the first downright dullness. By this time his readers had become familiar with his machinery and his materials—his elbowing suffragettes, his tea-swilling London uplifters, his smattering of quasi-science, his intellectualized adulteries, his Thackerayan asides, his text-book paragraphs, his journalistic raciness— and all these things had thus begun to lose the blush of their first charm. To help them out he heaved in larger and larger doses of theory—often diverting enough, and sometimes even persuasive, but in the long run a poor substitute for the proper ingredients of character, situation and human passion. Next came "The Wife of Sir Isaac Harman," an attempt to rewrite "A Doll's House" (with a fourth act) in

terms of ante-bellum 1914. The result was 500-odd
pages of bosh, a flabby and tedious piece of work,
Wells for the first time in the rôle of unmistakable
bore. And then "Bealby," with its Palais Royal jocosity, its running in and out of doors, its humor of
physical collision, its reminiscences of "A Trip to
Chinatown" and "Peck's Bad Boy." And then
"Boon," a heavy-witted satire, often incomprehensible, always incommoded by its disguise as a novel.
And then "The Research Magnificent": a poor soup
from the dry bones of Nietzsche. And then "Mr.
Britling Sees It Through" . . .

Here, for a happy moment, there seemed to be
something better—almost, in fact, a recrudescence of
the Wells of 1910. But that seeming was only seeming. What confused the judgment was the enormous
popular success of the book. Because it presented
a fifth-rate Englishman in an heroic aspect, because
it sentimentalized the whole reaction of the English
proletariat to the war, it offered a subtle sort of flat-
tery to other fifth-rate Englishmen, and, *per corollary*,
to Americans of corresponding degree, to wit, the second. Thus it made a great pother, and was hymned
as a masterpiece in such gazettes as the New York
Times, as Blasco Ibáñez's "The Four Horsemen of
the Apocalypse" was destined to be hymned three
years later. But there was in the book, in point of
fact, a great hollowness, and that hollowness presently

begat an implosion that disposed of the shell. I daresay many a novel-reader returns, now and then, to "Tono-Bungay," and even to "Ann Veronica." But surely only a reader with absolutely nothing else to read would return to "Mr. Britling Sees It Through." There followed—what? "The Soul of a Bishop," perhaps the worst novel ever written by a serious novelist since novel-writing began. And then—or perhaps a bit before, or simultaneously—an idiotic religious tract—a tract so utterly feeble and preposterous that even the Scotchman, William Archer, could not stomach it. And then, to make an end, came "Joan and Peter"—and the collapse of Wells was revealed at last in its true proportions.

This "Joan and Peter" I confess, lingers in my memory as unpleasantly as a summer cold, and so, in retrospect, I may perhaps exaggerate its intrinsic badness. I would not look into it again for gold and frankincense. I was at the job of reading it for days and days, endlessly daunted and halted by its laborious dullness, its flatulent fatuity, its almost fabulous inconsequentiality. It was, and is, nearly impossible to believe that the Wells of "Tono-Bungay" and "The History of Mr. Polly" wrote it, or that he was in the full possession of his faculties when he allowed it to be printed under his name. For in it there is the fault that the Wells of those days, almost beyond any other fictioneer of the time, was incapable of—

the fault of dismalness, of tediousness—the witless
and contagious coma of the evangelist. Here, for
nearly six hundred pages of fine type, he rolls on
in an intellectual cloud, boring one abominably with
uninteresting people, pointless situations, revelations
that reveal nothing, arguments that have no apposite-
ness, expositions that expose naught save an insatiable
and torturing garrulity. Where is the old fine address of the man? Where is his sharp eye for the
salient and significant in character? Where is his
instinct for form, his skill at putting a story together,
his hand for making it unwind itself? These things
are so far gone that it becomes hard to believe that
they ever existed. There is not the slightest sign of
them in "Joan and Peter." The book is a botch from
end to end, and in that botch there is not even the
palliation of an arduous enterprise gallantly attempted. No inherent difficulty is visible. The
story is anything but complex, and surely anything but
subtle. Its badness lies wholly in the fact that the
author made a mess of the writing, that his quondam
cunning, once so exhilarating, was gone when he began it.

Reviewing it at the time of its publication, I inclined momentarily to the notion that the war was to
blame. No one could overestimate the cost of that
struggle to the English, not only in men and money,
but also and more importantly in the things of the

spirit. It developed national traits that were greatly
at odds with the old ideal of Anglo-Saxon character
—an extravagant hysteria, a tendency to whimper
under blows, political radicalism and credulity. It
overthrew the old ruling caste of the land and gave
over the control of things to upstarts from the lowest
classes—shady Jews, snuffling Methodists, prehensile
commercial gents, disgusting demagogues, all sorts
of self-seeking adventurers. Worst of all, the strain
seemed to work havoc with the customary dignity and
reticence, and even with the plain commonsense of
many Englishmen on a higher level, and in particular many English writers. The astounding bawling
of Kipling and the no less astounding bombast of G.
K. Chesterton were anything but isolated; there were,
in fact, scores of other eminent authors in the same
state of eruption, and a study of the resultant literature of objurgation will make a fascinating job for
some sweating *Privatdozent* of to-morrow, say out of
Göttingen or Jena. It occurred to me, as I say, that
Wells might have become afflicted by this same de-
moralization, but reflection disposed of the notion.
On the one hand, there was the plain fact that his actual writings on the war, while marked by the bitter-
ness of the time, were anything but insane, and on
the other hand there was the equally plain fact that his
decay had been in progress a long while before the
Germans made their fateful thrust at Liége.

The precise thing that ailed him I found at last on page 272 *et seq.* of the American edition of his book. There it was plainly described, albeit unwittingly, but if you will go back to the other novels since "Marriage" you will find traces of it in all of them, and even more vivid indications in the books of exposition and philosophizing that have accompanied them. What has slowly crippled him and perhaps disposed of him is his gradual acceptance of the theory, corrupting to the artist and scarcely less so to the man, that he is one of the Great Thinkers of his era, charged with a pregnant Message to the Younger Generation—that his ideas, rammed into enough skulls, will Save the Empire, not only from the satanic Nietzscheism of the Hindenburgs and post-Hindenburgs, but also from all those inner Weaknesses that taint and flabbergast its vitals, as the tapeworm with nineteen heads devoured Atharippus of Macedon. In brief, he suffers from a messianic delusion—and once a man begins to suffer from a messianic delusion his days as a serious artist are ended. He may yet serve the state with laudable devotion; he may yet enchant his millions; he may yet posture and gyrate before the world as a man of mark. But not in the character of artist. Not as a creator of sound books. Not in the separate place of one who observes the eternal tragedy of man with full sympathy and understanding, and yet with a touch of god-like remoteness. Not as Homer saw it, smiting the while his blooming lyre.

I point, as I say, to page 272 of "Joan and Peter," whereon, imperfectly concealed by jocosity, you will find Wells' private view of Wells—a view at once too flattering and libelous. What it shows is the absorption of the artist in the tin-pot reformer and professional wise man. A descent, indeed! The man impinged upon us and made his first solid success, not as a merchant of banal pedagogics, not as a hawker of sociological liver-pills, but as a master of brilliant and life-like representation, an evoker of unaccustomed but none the less deep-seated emotions, a dramatist of fine imagination and highly resourceful execution. It was the stupendous drama and spectacle of modern life, and not its dubious and unintelligible lessons, that drew him from his test-tubes and guinea-pigs and made an artist of him, and to the business of that artist, once he had served his apprenticeship, he brought a vision so keen, a point of view so fresh and sane and a talent for exhibition so lively and original that he straightway conquered all of us. Nothing could exceed the sheer radiance of "Tono-Bungay." It is a work that glows with reality. It projects a whole epoch with unforgettable effect. It is a moving-picture conceived and arranged, not by the usual ex-bartender or chorus man, but by an extremely civilized and sophisticated ob-

server, alert to every detail of the surface and yet
acutely aware of the internal play of forces, the essential springs, the larger, deeper lines of it.   In
brief, it is a work of art of the soundest merit, for it
both represents accurately and interprets convincingly,
and under everything is a current of feeling that co-
ordinates and informs the whole.

But in the success of the book and of the two or
three following it there was a temptation, and in the
temptation a peril.   The audience was there, high
in expectation, eagerly demanding more.   And in the
ego of the man—a true proletarian, and hence born
with morals, faiths, certainties, vasty gaseous hopes
—there was an urge.   That urge, it seems to me, began to torture him when he set about "The Passionate Friends."   In the presence of it, he was dissuaded
from the business of an artist,—made discontented
with the business of an artist.   It was not enough to
display the life of his time with accuracy and understanding; it was not even enough to criticize it with
a penetrating humor and sagacity.   From the depths
of his being, like some foul miasma, there arose the
old, fatuous yearning to change it, to improve it, to
set it right where it was wrong, to make it over according to some pattern superior to the one followed by
the Lord God Jehovah.   With this sinister impulse,
as aberrant in an artist as a taste for legs in an arch-
bishop, the instinct that had created "Tono-Bungay"

and "The New Machiavelli" gave battle, and for a while the issue was in doubt. But with "Marriage," its trend began to be apparent—and before long the evangelist was triumphant, and his bray battered the ear, and in the end there was a quite different Wells before us, and a Wells worth infinitely less than the one driven off. To-day one must put him where he has begun to put himself—not among the literary artists of English, but among the brummagem prophets of England. His old rival was Arnold Bennett. His new rival is the Fabian Society, or maybe Lord Northcliffe, or the surviving Chesterton, or the later Hillaire Belloc.

The prophesying business is like writing fugues; it is fatal to every one save the man of absolute genius. The lesser fellow—and Wells, for all his cleverness, is surely one of the lesser fellows—is bound to come to grief at it, and one of the first signs of his coming to grief is the drying up of his sense of humor. Compare "The Soul of a Bishop" or "Joan and Peter" to "Ann Veronica" or "The History of Mr. Polly." One notices instantly the disappearance of the comic spirit, the old searching irony—in brief, of the precise thing that keeps the breath of life in Arnold Bennett. It was in "Boon," I believe, that this irony showed its last flare. There is a passage in that book which somehow lingers in the memory: a portrait of the United States as it arose in the mind of an Englishman reading the *Nation* of yesteryear: "a vain, garrulous and prosperous female of uncertain age, and still more uncertain temper, with unfounded pretensions to intellectuality and an idea of refinement of the most negative description . . . the Aunt Errant of Christendom." A capital whimsy—but blooming almost alone. A sense of humor, had it been able to survive the theology, would certainly have saved us from Lady Sunderbund, in "The Soul of a Bishop," and from Lady Charlotte Sydenham in "Joan and Peter." But it did not and could not survive. It always withers in the presence of the messianic delusion, like justice and the truth in front of patriotic passion. What takes its place is the oafish, witless buffoonishness of the chautauquas and the floor of Congress—for example, the sort of thing that makes an intolerable bore of "Bealby."

Nor are Wells' ideas, as he has so laboriously expounded them, worth the sacrifice of his old lively charm. They are, in fact, second-hand, and he often muddles them in the telling. In "First and Last Things" he preaches a flabby Socialism, and then, toward the end, admits frankly that it doesn't work. In "Boon" he erects a whole book upon an eighth-rate platitude, to wit, the platitude that English literature, in these latter times, is platitudinous—a three-cornered banality, indeed, for his own argument is a case in point, and so helps to prove what was al-

ready obvious. In "The Research Magnificent" he
smouches an idea from Nietzsche, and then mauls it so
badly that one begins to wonder whether he is in
favor of it or against it. In "The Undying Fire"
he first states the obvious, and then flees from it in
alarm. In his war books he borrows right and
left—from Dr. Wilson, from the British Socialists,
from Romain Rolland, even from such profound
thinkers as James M. Beck, Lloyd-George and the
editor of the New York *Tribune*—and everything
that he borrows is flat. In "Joan and Peter" he first
argues that England is going to pot because English education is too formal and archaic, and then
that Germany is going to pot because German education is too realistic and opportunist. He seems to
respond to all the varying crazes and fallacies of the
day; he swallows them without digesting them; he
tries to substitute mere timeliness for reflection and
feeling. And under all the rumble-bumble of bad
ideas is the imbecile assumption of the jitney messiah
at all times and everywhere: that human beings may
be made over by changing the rules under which they
live, that progress is a matter of intent and foresight,
that an act of Parliament can cure the blunders and
check the practical joking of God.

Such notions are surely no baggage for a serious
novelist. A novelist, of course, must have a point
of view, but it must be a point of view untroubled by

the crazes of the moment, it must regard the internal
workings and meanings of existence and not merely
its superficial appearances.   A novelist must view life
from some secure rock, drawing it into a definite per-
spective, interpreting it upon an ordered plan.   Even
if he hold (as Conrad does, and Dreiser, and Hardy,
and Anatole France) that it is essentially meaningless, he must at least display that meaninglessness
with reasonable clarity and consistency.   Wells shows
no such solid and intelligible attitude.   He is too
facile, too enthusiastic, too eager to teach to-day what
he learned yesterday.   Van Wyck Brooks once tried
to reduce the whole body of his doctrine to a succinct
statement.   The result was a little volume a great
deal more plausible than any that Wells himself has
ever written—but also one that probably surprised
him now and then as he read it.   In it all his contradictions were reconciled, all his gaps bridged, all his
shifts ameliorated.   Brooks did for him, in brief,
what William Bayard Hale did for Dr. Wilson in
"The New Freedom," and has lived to regret it, I
daresay, or at all events the vain labor of it, in the
same manner. . . .

What remains of Wells?   There remains a little
shelf of very excellent books, beginning with "Tono-
Bungay" and ending with "Marriage."   It is a shelf
flanked on the one side by a long row of extravagant
romances in the manner of Jules Verne, and on the

other side by an even longer row of puerile tracts. But let us not underestimate it because it is in such uninviting company.   There is on it some of the liveliest, most original, most amusing, and withal most respectable fiction that England has produced in our time.   In that fiction there is a sufficient memorial to a man who, between two debauches of claptrap, had his day as an artist.

III. ARNOLD BENNETT

OF Bennett it is quite easy to conjure up a recognizable picture by imaging everything that Wells is not—that is, everything interior, everything having to do with attitudes and ideas, everything beyond the mere craft of arranging words in ingratiating sequences. As stylists, of course, they have many points of contact. Each writes a journalese that is extraordinarily fluent and tuneful; each is apt to be carried away by the rush of his own smartness. But in their matter they stand at opposite poles. Wells has a believing mind, and cannot resist the lascivious beckonings and eye-winkings of meretricious novelty; Bennett carries skepticism so far that it often takes on the appearance of a mere peasant-like suspicion of ideas, bellicose and unintelligent. Wells is astonishingly intimate and confidential; and more than one of his novels reeks with a shameless sort of autobiography; Bennett, even when he makes use of personal experience, contrives to get impersonality into it. Wells, finally, is a sentimentalist, and cannot conceal his feelings; Bennett, of all the English novelists of the day, is the most steadily aloof and ironical.

36

This habit of irony, in truth, is the thing that gives Bennett all his characteristic color, and is at the bottom of both his peculiar merit and his peculiar limitation. On the one hand it sets him free from the besetting sin of the contemporary novelist: he never preaches, he has no messianic delusion, he is above the puerile theories that have engulfed such romantic men as Wells, Winston Churchill and the late Jack London, and even, at times, such sentimental agnostics as Dreiser. But on the other hand it leaves him empty of the passion that is, when all is said and done, the chief mark of the true novelist. The trouble with him is that he cannot feel with his characters, that he never involves himself emotionally in their struggles against destiny, that the drama of their lives never thrills or dismays him—and the result is that he is unable to arouse in the reader that penetrating sense of kinship, that profound and instinctive sympathy, which in its net effect is almost indistinguishable from the understanding born of experiences actually endured and emotions actually shared. Joseph Conrad, in a memorable piece of criticism, once put the thing clearly. "My task," he said, "is, by the power of the written word, to make you hear, to make you feel — it is, above all, to make you *see*." Here seeing, it must be obvious, is no more than feeling put into physical terms; it is not the outward aspect that is to be seen, but the inner truth—and the end to be sought by that apprehension of inner truth is responsive recognition, the sympathy of poor mortal for poor mortal, the tidal uprush of feeling that makes us all one. Bennett, it seems to me, cannot evoke it. His characters, as they pass, have a deceptive brilliance of outline, but they soon fade; one never finds them haunting the memory as Lord Jim haunts it, or Carrie Meeber, or Huck Finn, or Tom Jones. The reason is not far to seek. It lies in the plain fact that they appear to their creator, not as men and women whose hopes and agonies are of poignant concern, not as tragic comedians in isolated and concentrated dramas, but as mean figures in an infinitely dispersed and unintelligible farce, as helpless nobodies in an epic struggle that transcends both their volition and their comprehension. Thus viewing them, he fails to humanize them completely, and so he fails to make their emotions contagious. They are, in their way, often vividly real; they are thoroughly accounted for; what there is of them is unfailingly life-like; they move and breathe in an environment that pulses and glows. But the attitude of the author toward them remains, in the end, the attitude of a biologist toward his laboratory animals. He does not *feel* with them —and neither does his reader.

Bennett's chief business, in fact, is not with individuals at all, even though he occasionally brings them up almost to life-size. What concerns him princi-

pally is the common life of large groups, the action
and reaction of castes and classes, the struggle among
societies. In particular, he is engrossed by the colossal and disorderly functioning of the English middle
class—a division of mankind inordinately mixed in
race, confused in ideals and illogical in ideas. It is
a group that has had interpreters aplenty, past and
present; a full half of the literature of the Victorian
era was devoted to it. But never, I believe, has it
had an interpreter more resolutely detached and relentless—never has it had one less shaken by emotional involvement. Here the very lack that detracts
so much from Bennett's stature as a novelist in the
conventional sense is converted into a valuable possession. Better than any other man of his time he has
got upon paper the social anatomy and physiology of
the masses of average, everyday, unimaginative Englishmen. One leaves the long series of Five Towns
books with a sense of having looked down the tube
of a microscope upon a huge swarm of infinitely little but incessantly struggling organisms—creatures
engaged furiously in the pursuit of grotesque and
unintelligible ends—helpless participants in and victims of a struggle that takes on, to their eyes, a thousand lofty purposes, all of them puerile to the observer
above its turmoil. Here, he seems to say, is the middle, the average, the typical Englishman. Here is the
fellow as he appears to himself—virtuous, laborious,

important, intelligent, made in God's image. And here he is in fact—swinish, ineffective, inconsequential, stupid, a feeble parody upon his maker. It is irony that penetrates and devastates, and it is unrelieved by any show of the pity that gets into the irony of Conrad, or of the tolerant claim of kinship that mitigates that of Fielding and Thackeray. It is harsh and cocksure. It has, at its moments, some flavor of actual bounderism: one instinctively shrinks from so smart-alecky a pulling off of underclothes and unveiling of warts.

It is easy to discern in it, indeed, a note of distinct hostility, and even of disgust. The long exile of the author is not without its significance. He not only got in France something of the Frenchman's aloof and disdainful view of the English; he must have taken a certain distaste for the national scene with him in the first place, else he would not have gone at all. The same attitude shows itself in W. L. George, another Englishman smeared with Gallic foreignness. Both men, it will be recalled, reacted to the tremendous emotional assault of the war, not by yielding to it ecstatically in the manner of the unpolluted islanders, but by shrinking from it into a reserve that was naturally misunderstood. George has put his sniffs into "Blind Alley"; Bennett has got his into "The Pretty Lady." I do not say that either book is positively French; what I do say is that both mirror an attitude that has been somehow emptied of mere nationalism. An Italian adventure, I daresay, would have produced the same effect, or a Spanish, or Russian, or German. But it happened to be French. What the Bennett story attempts to do is what every serious Bennett story attempts to do: to exhibit dramatically the great gap separating the substance from the appearance in the English character. It seems to me that its prudent and self-centered G. J. Hoape is a vastly more real Englishman of his class, and, what is more, an Englishman vastly more useful and creditable to England, than any of the gaudy Bayards and Cids of conventional war fiction. Here, indeed, the irony somehow fails. The man we are obviously expected to disdain converts himself, toward the end, into a man not without his touches of the admirable. He is no hero, God knows, and there is no more brilliance in him than you will find in an average country squire or Parliament man, but he has the rare virtue of common sense, and that is probably the virtue that has served the English better than all others. Curiously enough, the English reading public recognized the irony but failed to observe its confutation, and so the book got Bennett into bad odor at home, and into worse odor among the sedulous apes of English ideas and emotions on this side of the water. But it is a sound work nevertheless—a sound work with a large and unescapable defect.

That defect is visible in a good many of the other
things that Bennett has done.   It is the product of his
emotional detachment and it commonly reveals itself
as an inability to take his own story seriously.   Sometimes he pokes open fun at it, as in "The Roll-Call";
more often he simply abandons it before it is done,
as if weary of a too tedious foolery.   This last process
is plainly visible in "The Pretty Lady."   The thing
that gives form and direction to that story is a simple
enough problem in psychology, to wit: what will
happen when a man of sound education and decent
instincts, of sober age and prudent habit, of common
sense and even of certain mild cleverness—what will
happen, logically and naturally, when such a normal,
respectable, cautious fellow finds himself disquiet-
ingly in love with a lady of no position at all—in
brief, with a lady but lately of the town?   Bennett
sets the problem, and for a couple of hundred pages
investigates it with the utmost ingenuity and address,
exposing and discussing its sub-problems, tracing the
gradual shifting of its terms, prodding with sharp in-
sight into the psychological material entering into it.
And then, as if suddenly tired of it—worse, as if suddenly convinced that the thing has gone on long enough,
that he has given the public enough of a book for
its money—he forthwith evades the solution altogether, and brings down his curtain upon a palpably
artificial dénouement.   The device murders the book.

One is arrested at the start by a fascinating statement of the problem, one follows a discussion of
it that shows Bennett at his brilliant best, fertile
in detail, alert to every twist of motive, incisively
ironical at every step—and then, at the end, one is
incontinently turned out of the booth. The effect is
that of being assaulted with an ice-pick by a hitherto
amiable bartender, almost that of being bitten by a
pretty girl in the midst of an amicable buss.

That effect, unluckily, is no stranger to the reader
of Bennett novels. One encounters it in many of
them. There is a tremendous marshaling of meticulous and illuminating observation, the background
throbs with color, the sardonic humor is never failing,
it is a capital show—but always one goes away from
it with a sense of having missed the conclusion, always there is a final begging of the question. It is
not hard to perceive the attitude of mind underlying
this chronic evasion of issues. It is, in essence, agnosticism carried to the last place of decimals. Life
itself is meaningless; therefore, the discussion of life
is meaningless; therefore, why try futilely to get a
meaning into it? The reasoning, unluckily, has holes
in it. It may be sound logically, but it is psycho-
logically unworkable. One goes to novels, not for the
bald scientific fact, but for a romantic amelioration of
it. When they carry that amelioration to the point
of uncritical certainty, when they are full of "ideas"

that click and whirl like machines, then the mind re-
volts against the childish naïveté of the thing. But
when there is no organization of the spectacle at all,
when it is presented as a mere formless panorama,
when to the sense of its unintelligibility is added the
suggestion of its inherent chaos, then the mind re-
volts no less. Art can never be simple representation. It cannot deal solely with precisely what is. It
must, at the least, present the real in the light of some
recognizable ideal; it must give to the eternal farce, if
not some moral, then at all events some direction.
For without that formulation there can be no clear-
cut separation of the individual will from the general stew and turmoil of things, and without that separation there can be no coherent drama, and without
that drama there can be no evocation of emotion, and
without that emotion art is unimaginable. The field
of the novel is very wide. There is room, on the one
side, for a brilliant play of ideas and theories, provided only they do not stiffen the struggle of man with
man, or of man with destiny, into a mere struggle of
abstractions. There is room, on the other side, for
the most complete agnosticism, provided only it be
tempered by feeling. Joseph Conrad is quite as unshakable an agnostic as Bennett; he is a ten times more
implacable ironist. But there is yet a place in his
scheme for a sardonic sort of pity, and pity, however
sardonic, is perhaps as good an emotion as another.

The trouble with Bennett is that he essays to sneer, not only at the futile aspiration of man, but also at the agony that goes with it. The result is an air of affectation, of superficiality, almost of stupidity. The manner, on the one hand, is that of a highly skillful and profoundly original artist, but on the other hand it is that of a sophomore just made aware of Haeckel, Bradlaugh and Nietzsche.

Bennett's unmitigated skepticism explains two things that have constantly puzzled the reviewers, and that have been the cause of a great deal of idiotic writing about him—for him as well as against him. One of these things is his utter lack of anything properly describable as artistic conscience—his extreme readiness to play the star houri in the seraglio of the publishers; the other is his habit of translating platitudes into racy journalese and gravely offering them to the suburban trade as "pocket philosophies." Both crimes, it seems to me, have their rise in his congenital incapacity for taking ideas seriously, even including his own. "If this," he appears to say, "is the tosh you want, then here is another dose of it. Personally, I have little interest in that sort of thing. Even good novels—the best I can do—are no more than compromises with a silly convention. I am not interested in stories; I am interested in the anatomy of human melancholy; I am a descriptive sociologist, with overtones of malice. But if you want stories, and can pay for them, I am willing to give them to you. And if you prefer bad stories, then here is a bad one. Don't assume you can shame me by deploring my willing-ness. Think of what your doctors do every day, and your lawyers, and your men of God, and your stock-brokers, and your traders and politicians. I am surely no worse than the average. In fact, I am prob-ably a good deal superior to the average, for I am at least not deceived by my own mountebankery—I at least know my sound goods from my shoddy." Such, I daresay, is the process of thought behind such hol-low trade-goods as "Buried Alive" and "The Lion's Share." One does not need the man's own amazing confidences to hear his snickers at his audience, at his work and at himself.

The books of boiled-mutton "philosophy" in the manner of Dr. Orison Swett Marden and Dr. Frank Crane and the occasional pot-boilers for the news-papers and magazines probably have much the same origin. What appears in them is not a weakness for ideas that are stale and obvious, but a distrust of all ideas whatsoever. The public, with its mob yearning to be instructed, edified and pulled by the nose, de-mands certainties; it must be told definitely and a bit raucously that this is true and that is false. But there *are* no certainties. *Ergo,* one notion is as good as another, and if it happens to be utter flubdub, so much the better—for it is precisely flubdub that penetrates

the popular skull with the greatest facility. The way
is already made: the hole already gapes. An effort
to approach the hidden and baffling truth would simply
burden the enterprise with difficulty. Moreover, the
effort is intrinsically laborious and ungrateful. Moreover, there is probably no hidden truth to be uncov-
ered. Thus, by the route of skepticism, Bennett apparently arrives at his sooth-saying. That he actually believes in his own theorizing is inconceivable.
He is far too intelligent a man to hold that any truths
within the comprehension of the popular audience are
sound enough to be worth preaching, or that it would
do any good to preach them if they were. No doubt
he is considerably amused *in petto* by the gravity with
which his bedizened platitudes have been received by
persons accustomed to that sort of fare, particularly
in America. It would be interesting to hear his private view of the corn-fed critics who hymn him as a
profound and impassioned moralist, with a mission to
rescue the plain people from the heresies of such fellows as Dreiser.

So much for two of the salient symptoms of his
underlying skepticism. Another is to be found in his
incapacity to be, in the ordinary sense, ingratiating;
it is simply beyond him to say the pleasant thing
with any show of sincerity. Of all his books, probably the worst are his book on the war and his book
on the United States. The latter was obviously un-

dertaken with some notion of paying off a debt. Bennett had been to the United States; the newspapers
had hailed him in their side-show way; the women's
clubs had pawed over him; he had, no doubt, come
home a good deal richer. What he essayed to do was
to write a volume on the republic that should be at
once colorably accurate and discreetly agreeable.
The enterprise was quite beyond him. The book not
only failed to please Americans; it offended them in
a thousand subtle ways, and from its appearance
dates the decline of the author's vogue among us. He
is not, of course, completely forgotten, but it must be
plain that Wells now stands a good deal above him in
the popular estimation—even the later Wells of bad
novel after bad novel. His war book missed fire in
much the same way. It was workmanlike, it was deliberately urbane, it was undoubtedly truthful—but it
fell flat in England and it fell flat in America. There
is no little significance in the fact that the British
government, in looking about for English authors
to uphold the British cause in America and labor for
American participation in the war, found no usefulness in Bennett. Practically every other novelist
with an American audience was drafted for service,
but not Bennett. He was *non est* during the heat of
the fray, and when at length he came forward with
"The Pretty Lady" the pained manner with which it

was received quite justified the judgment of those who
had passed him over.

What all this amounts to may be very briefly put: in
one of the requisite qualities of the first-rate novelist
Bennett is almost completely lacking, and so it would
be no juggling with paradox to argue that, at bottom,
he is scarcely a novelist at all. His books, indeed,—
that is, his serious books, the books of his better canon
—often fail utterly to achieve the effect that one associates with the true novel. One carries away from
them, not the impression of a definite transaction, not
the memory of an outstanding and appealing personality, not the after-taste of a profound emotion, but
merely the sense of having witnessed a gorgeous but
incomprehensible parade, coming out of nowhere and
going to God knows where. They are magnificent as
representation, they bristle with charming detail, they
radiate the humors of an acute and extraordinary man,
they are entertainment of the best sort—but there is
seldom anything in them of that clear, well-aimed
and solid effect which one associates with the novel
as work of art. Most of these books, indeed, are no
more than collections of essays defectively dramatized.
What is salient in them is not their people, but their
backgrounds—and their people are forever fading
into their backgrounds. Is there a character in any
of these books that shows any sign of living as Pen-

dennis lives, and Barry Lyndon, and Emma Bovary, and David Copperfield, and the George Moore who is always his own hero? Who remembers much about Sophia Baines, save that she lived in the Five Towns, or even about Clayhanger? Young George Cannon, in "The Roll-Call," is no more than an anatomical chart in a lecture on modern marriage. Hilda Lessways-Cannon-Clayhanger is not only inscrutable; she is also dim. The man and woman of "Whom God Hath Joined," perhaps the best of all the Bennett novels, I have so far forgotten that I cannot remember their names. Even Denry the Audacious grows misty. One remembers that he was the center of the farce, but now he is long gone and the farce remains.

This constant remainder, whether he be actually novelist or no novelist, is sufficient to save Bennett, it seems to me, from the swift oblivion that so often overtakes the popular fictioneer. He may not play the game according to the rules, but the game that he plays is nevertheless extraordinarily diverting and calls for an incessant display of the finest sort of skill. No writer of his time has looked into the life of his time with sharper eyes, or set forth his findings with a greater charm and plausibility. Within his deliberately narrow limits he had done precisely the thing that Balzac undertook to do, and Zola after him: he has painted a full-length portrait of a whole society, accurately, brilliantly and, in certain areas, almost exhaustively. The middle Englishman—not the individual, but the type—is there displayed more vividly than he is displayed anywhere else that I know of. The thing is rigidly held to its aim; there is no episodic descent or ascent to other fields. But within that one field every resource of observation, of invention and of imagination has been brought to bear upon the business—every one save that deep feeling for man in his bitter tragedy which is the most important of them all. Bennett, whatever his failing in this capital function of the artist, is certainly of the very highest consideration as craftsman. Scattered through his books, even his bad books, there are fragments of writing that are quite unsurpassed in our day—the shoe-shining episode in "The Pretty Lady," the adulterous interlude in "Whom God Hath Joined," the dinner party in "Paris Nights," the whole discussion of the Cannon-Ingram marriage in "The Roll-Call," the studio party in "The Lion's Share." Such writing is rare and exhilarating. It is to be respected. And the man who did it is not to be dismissed.

IV. THE DEAN

AMERICANS, obsessed by the problem of conduct, usually judge their authors, not as artists, but as citizens, Christians, men. Edgar Allan Poe, I daresay, will never live down the fact that he was a periodical drunkard, and died in an alcoholic ward. Mark Twain, the incomparable artist, will probably never shake off Mark Twain, the after-dinner comedian, the flaunter of white dress clothes, the public character, the national wag. As for William Dean Howells, he gains rather than loses by this confusion of values, for, like the late Joseph H. Choate, he is almost the national ideal: an urbane and highly respectable old gentleman, a sitter on committees, an intimate of professors and the prophets of movements, a worthy vouched for by both the *Atlantic Monthly* and Alexander Harvey, a placid conformist. The result is his general acceptance as a member of the literary peerage, and of the rank of earl at least. For twenty years past his successive books have not been criticized, nor even adequately reviewed; they have been merely fawned over; the lady critics of the newspapers would no more question them than they would question Lincoln's Gettysburg speech, or Paul Elmer More, or their own virginity. The dean of American letters in point of years, and in point of published quantity, and in point of public prominence and influence, he has been gradually enveloped in a web of superstitious reverence, and it grates harshly to hear his actual achievement discussed in cold blood.

Nevertheless, all this merited respect for an industrious and inoffensive man is bound, soon or late, to yield to a critical examination of the artist within, and that examination, I fear, will have its bitter moments for those who naïvely accept the Howells legend. It will show, without doubt, a first-rate journeyman, a contriver of pretty things, a clever stylist —but it will also show a long row of uninspired and hollow books, with no more ideas in them than so many volumes of the *Ladies' Home Journal,* and no more deep and contagious feeling than so many reports of autopsies, and no more glow and gusto than so many tables of bond prices. The profound dread and agony of life, the surge of passion and aspiration, the grand crash and glitter of things, the tragedy that runs eternally under the surface—all this the critic of the future will seek in vain in Dr. Howells' elegant and shallow volumes. And seeking it in vain, he will probably dismiss all of them together with fewer words than he gives to "Huckleberry Finn." . . .

Already, indeed, the Howells legend tends to become a mere legend, and empty of all genuine significance. Who actually reads the Howells novels?
Who even remembers their names? "The Minister's
Charge," "An Imperative Duty," "The Unexpected
Guests," "Out of the Question," "No Love Lost"—
these titles are already as meaningless as a roll of
Sumerian kings. Perhaps "The Rise of Silas Lap-
ham" survives—but go read it if you would tumble
downstairs. The truth about Howells is that he
really has nothing to say, for all the charm he gets
into saying it. His psychology is superficial, amateurish, often nonsensical; his irony is scarcely more
than a polite facetiousness; his characters simply re-
fuse to live. No figure even remotely comparable to
Norris' McTeague or Dreiser's Frank Cowperwood
is to be encountered in his novels. He is quite un-
equal to any such evocation of the race-spirit, of the
essential conflict of forces among us, of the peculiar
drift and color of American life. The world he
moves in is suburban, caged, flabby. He could no
more have written the last chapters of "Lord Jim"
than he could have written the Book of Mark.

The vacuity of his method is well revealed by one
of the books of his old age,"The Leatherwood God."
Its composition, we are told, spread over many years;
its genesis was in the days of his full maturity. An
examination of it shows nothing but a suave piling

up of words, a vast accumulation of nothings. The central character, one Dylks, is a backwoods evangelist who acquires a belief in his own buncombe, and ends by announcing that he is God. The job before the author was obviously that of tracing the psychological steps whereby this mountebank proceeds to that conclusion; the fact, indeed, is recognized in the canned review, which says that the book is "a study of American religious psychology." But an inspection of the text shows that no such study is really in it. Dr. Howells does not *show* how Dylks came to believe himself God; he merely *says* that he did so. The whole discussion of the process, indeed, is confined to two pages—172 and 173—and is quite infantile in its inadequacy. Nor do we get anything approaching a revealing look into the heads of the other converts—the saleratus-sodden, hell-crazy, half-witted Methodists and Baptists of a remote Ohio settlement of seventy or eighty years ago. All we have is the casual statement that they are converted, and begin to offer Dylks their howls of devotion. And when, in the end, they go back to their original bosh, dethroning Dylks overnight and restoring the gaseous vertebrate of Calvin and Wesley—when this contrary process is recorded, it is accompanied by no more illumination. In brief, the story is not a "study" at all, whether psychological or otherwise, but simply an anecdote, and without either point or interest. Its

virtues are all negative ones: it is short, it keeps on
the track, it deals with a religious maniac and yet contrives to offer no offense to other religious maniacs.
But on the positive side it merely skims the skin.

So in all of the other Howells novels that I know.
Somehow, he seems blissfully ignorant that life is a
serious business, and full of mystery; it is a sort of
college town *Weltanschauung* that one finds in him;
he is an Agnes Repplier in pantaloons.   In one of the
later stories, "New Leaf Mills," he makes a faltering
gesture of recognition.   Here, so to speak, one gets
at least a sniff of the universal mystery; Howells seems
about to grow profound at last.   But the sniff is only
a sniff.   The tragedy, at the end, peters out.   Compare the story to E. W. Howe's "The Story of a Country Town," which Howells himself has intelligently
praised, and you will get some measure of his own
failure.   Howe sets much the same stage and deals
with much the same people.   His story is full of
technical defects—for one thing, it is overladen with
melodrama and sentimentality.   But nevertheless it
achieves the prime purpose of a work of the imagination: it grips and stirs the emotions, it implants a
sense of something experienced.   Such a book leaves
scars; one is not quite the same after reading it.   But
it would be difficult to point to a Howells book that
produces any such effect.   If he actually tries, like
Conrad, "to make you hear, to make you feel—be-

fore all, to make you *see*," then he fails almost completely. One often suspects, indeed, that he doesn't
really feel or see himself. . . .

As a critic he belongs to a higher level, if only because of his eager curiosity, his gusto in novelty.
His praise of Howe I have mentioned. He dealt
valiant licks for other débutantes: Frank Norris,
Edith Wharton and William Vaughn Moody among
them. He brought forward the Russians diligently
and persuasively, albeit they left no mark upon his
own manner. In his ingratiating way, back in the
seventies and eighties, he made war upon the prevailing sentimentalities. But his history as a critic
is full of errors and omissions. One finds him loos-
ing a fanfare for W. B. Trites, the Philadelphia Zola,
and praising Frank A. Munsey—and one finds him
leaving the discovery of all the Shaws, George
Moores, Dreisers, Synges, Galsworthys, Phillipses
and George Ades to the Pollards, Meltzers and Hu-
nekers. Busy in the sideshows, he didn't see the ele-
phants go by. . . . Here temperamental defects
handicapped him. Turn to his "My Mark Twain"
and you will see what I mean. The Mark that is exhibited in this book is a Mark whose Himalayan outlines are discerned but hazily through a pink fog of
Howells. There is a moral note in the tale—an obvious effort to palliate, to touch up, to excuse. The
poor fellow, of course, was charming, and there was

talent in him, but what a weakness he had for thinking aloud—and such shocking thoughts! What oaths
in his speech! What awful cigars he smoked!
How barbarous his contempt for the strict sonata
form! It seems incredible, indeed, that two men so
unlike should have found common denominators for
a friendship lasting forty-four years. The one derived from Rabelais, Chaucer, the Elizabethans and
Benvenuto—buccaneers of the literary high seas,
loud laughers, law-breakers, giants of a lordlier day;
the other came down from Jane Austen, Washington
Irving and Hannah More. The one wrote English
as Michelangelo hacked marble, broadly, brutally,
magnificently; the other was a maker of pretty waxen
groups. The one was utterly unconscious of the way
he achieved his staggering effects; the other was the
most toilsome, fastidious and self-conscious of craftsmen. . . .

What remains of Howells is his style. He invented a new harmony of "the old, old words." He
destroyed the stately periods of the Poe tradition, and
erected upon the ruins a complex and savory care-
lessness, full of naïvetés that were sophisticated to
the last degree. He loosened the tightness of English, and let a blast of Elizabethan air into it. He
achieved, for all his triviality, for all his narrowness
of vision, a pungent and admirable style.

V. PROFESSOR VEBLEN

TEN or twelve years ago, being engaged in a bombastic discussion with what was then known as an intellectual Socialist (like the rest of the *intelligentsia*, he succumbed to the first fife-corps of the war, pulled down the red flag, damned Marx as a German spy, and began whooping for Elihu Root, Otto Kahn and Abraham Lincoln), I was greatly belabored and incommoded by his long quotations from a certain Prof. Dr. Thorstein Veblen, then quite unknown to me. My antagonist manifestly attached a great deal of importance to these borrowed sagacities, for he often heaved them at me in lengths of a column or two, and urged me to read every word of them. I tried hard enough, but found it impossible going. The more I read them, in fact, the less I could make of them, and so in the end, growing impatient and impolite, I denounced this Prof. Veblen as a geyser of pishposh, refused to waste any more time upon his incomprehensible syllogisms, and applied myself to the other Socialist witnesses in the case, seeking to set fire to their shirts.

That old debate, which took place by mail (for the

Socialist lived like a munitions patriot on his country estate and I was a wage-slave attached to a city news-paper), was afterward embalmed in a dull book, and made the mild pother of a day. The book, by name, "Men vs. the Man," is now as completely forgotten as Baxter's "Saint's Rest" or the Constitution of the United States. I myself, perhaps the only man who remembers it at all, have not looked into it for six or eight years, and all I can recall of my opponent's argument (beyond the fact that it not only failed to convert me to the nascent Bolshevism of the time, but left me a bitter and incurable scoffer at democracy in all its forms) is his curious respect for the aforesaid Prof. Dr. Thorstein Veblen, and his delight in the learned gentleman's long, tortuous and (to me, at least) intolerably flapdoodlish phrases.

There was, indeed, a time when I forgot even this —when my mind was empty of the professor's very name. That was, say, from 1909 or thereabout to the middle of 1917. During those years, having lost all my old superior interest in Socialism, even as an amateur psychiatrist, I ceased to read its literature, and thus lost track of its Great Thinkers. The periodicals that I then gave an eye to, setting aside newspapers, were chiefly the familiar American imi-tations of the English weeklies of opinion, and in these the dominant Great Thinker was, first, the late Prof. Dr. William James, and, after his decease,

Prof. Dr. John Dewey. The reign of James, as the illuminated will recall, was long and glorious. For three or four years running he was mentioned in every one of those American *Spectators* and *Saturday Reviews* at least once a week, and often a dozen times. Among the less somber gazettes of the republic, to be sure, there were other heroes: Maeterlinck, Rabindranath Tagore, Judge Ben B. Lindsey, the late Major-General Roosevelt, Tom Lawson and so on. Still further down the literary and intellectual scale there were yet others: Hall Caine, Brieux and Jack Johnson among them, with paper-bag cookery and the twilight sleep to dispute their popularity. But on the majestic level of the old *Nation,* among the white and lavender peaks of professorial ratiocination, there was scarcely a serious rival to James. Now and then, perhaps, Jane Addams had a month of vogue, and during one winter there was a rage for Bergson, and for a short space the unspeakable Bernstorff tried to set up Eucken (now damned with Wagner, Nietzsche and Ludendorff), but taking one day with another James held his own against the field. His ideas, immediately they were stated, became the ideas of every pedagogue from Harvard to Leland Stanford, and the pedagogues, laboring furiously at space rates, rammed them into the skulls of the lesser *cerebelli.* To have called James an ass, during the year 1909, would have been as fatal as to have written a sentence

like this one without having used so many *haves*.
He died a bit later, but his ghost went marching on:
it took three or four years to interpret and pigeon-
hole his philosophical remains and to take down and
redact his messages (via Sir Oliver Lodge, Little
Brighteyes, Wah-Wah the Indian Chief, and other
gifted psychics) from the spirit world. But then,
gradually, he achieved the ultimate, stupendous and
irrevocable act of death, and there was a vacancy.
To it Prof. Dr. Dewey was elected by the acclamation
of all right-thinking and forward-looking men. He
was an expert in pedagogics, metaphysics, psychology,
ethics, logic, politics, pedagogical metaphysics, meta-
physical psychology, psychological ethics, ethical
logic, logical politics and political pedagogics. He
was *Artium Magister, Philosophiæ Doctor* and twice
Legum Doctor. He had written a book called "How
to Think." He sat in a professor's chair and caned
sophomores for blowing spit-balls. *Ergo,* he was the
ideal candidate, and so he was nominated, elected and
inaugurated, and for three years, more or less, he enjoyed a peaceful reign in the groves of sapience, and
the inferior *umbilicarii* venerated him as they had
once venerated James.

I myself greatly enjoyed and profited by the dis-
courses of this Prof. Dewey and was in hopes that he
would last. Born so recently as 1859 and a man of
the highest bearable sobriety, he seemed likely to peg

along until 1935 or 1940, a gentle and charming volcano of correct thought. But it was not, alas, to be. Under cover of pragmatism, that serpent's metaphysic, there was unrest beneath the surface. Young professors in remote and obscure universities, apparently as harmless as so many convicts in the death-house, were secretly flirting with new and red-hot ideas. Whole regiments and brigades of them yielded in stealthy privacy to rebellious and often incomprehensible yearnings. Now and then, as if to reveal what was brewing, a hell fire blazed and a Prof. Dr. Scott Nearing went sky-hooting through its smoke. One heard whispers of strange heresies—economic, sociological, even political. Gossip had it that pedagogy was hatching vipers, nay, was already brought to bed. But not much of this got into the home-made *Saturday Reviews* and Yankee *Athenæums*—a hint or two maybe, but no more. In the main they kept to their old resolute demands for a pure civil-service, the budget system in Congress, the abolition of hazing at the Naval Academy, an honest primary and justice to the Filipinos, with extermination of the Prussian serpent added after August, 1914. And Dr. Dewey, on his remote Socratic Alp, pursued the calm reënforcement of the philosophical principles underlying these and all other lofty and indignant causes. . . .

Then, of a sudden, Siss! Boom! Ah! Then,

overnight, the upspringing of the intellectual soviets, the headlong assault upon all the old axioms of pedagogical speculation, the nihilistic dethronement of Prof. Dewey—and rah, rah, rah for Prof. Dr. Thorstein Veblen! Veblen? Could it be—? Aye, it was! My old acquaintance! The *Doctor obscurus* of my half-forgotten bout with the so-called intellectual Socialist! The Great Thinker *redivivus!* Here, indeed, he was again, and in a few months— almost it seemed a few days—he was all over the *Nation,* the *Dial,* the *New Republic* and the rest of them, and his books and pamphlets began to pour from the presses, and the newspapers reported his every wink and whisper, and everybody who was anybody began gabbling about him. The spectacle, I do not hesitate to say, somewhat disconcerted me and even distressed me. On the one hand, I was sorry to see so learned and interesting a man as Dr. Dewey sent back to the insufferable dungeons of Columbia, there to lecture in imperfect Yiddish to classes of Grand Street Platos. And on the other hand, I shrunk supinely from the appalling job, newly rearing itself before me, of re-reading the whole canon of the singularly laborious and muggy, the incomparably tangled and unintelligible works of Prof. Dr. Thorstein Veblen. . . .

But if a sense of duty tortures a man, it also enables him to achieve prodigies, and so I managed to get through the whole infernal job. I read "The Theory of the Leisure Class," I read "The Theory of Business Enterprise," and then I read "The Instinct of Workmanship." An hiatus followed; I was racked by a severe neuralgia, with delusions of persecution. On recovering I tackled "Imperial Germany and the Industrial Revolution." Malaria for a month, and then "The Nature of Peace and the Terms of Its Perpetuation." What ensued was never diagnosed; probably it was some low infection of the mesentery or spleen. When it passed off, leaving only an asthmatic cough, I read "The Higher Learning in America," and then went to Mt. Clemens to drink the Glauber's salts. Eureka! the business was done! It had strained me, but now it was over. Alas, a good part of the agony had been needless. What I found myself aware of, coming to the end, was that practically the whole system of Prof. Dr. Veblen was in his first book and his last—that is, in "The Theory of the Leisure Class," and "The Higher Learning in America." I pass on the good news. Read these two, and you won't have to read the others. And if even two daunt you, then read the first. Once through it, though you will have missed many a pearl and many a pain, you will have a fairly good general acquaintance with the gifted metaphysician's ideas.

For those ideas, in the main, are quite simple, and often anything but revolutionary in essence. What

is genuinely remarkable about them is not their novelty, or their complexity, nor even the fact that a professor should harbor them; it is the astoundingly
grandiose and rococo manner of their statement, the
almost unbelievable tediousness and flatulence of the
gifted headmaster's prose, his unprecedented talent
for saying nothing in an august and heroic manner.
There are tales of an actress of the last generation,
probably Sarah Bernhardt, who could put pathos and
even terror into a recitation of the multiplication table.
The late Louis James did something of the sort; he
introduced limericks into "Peer Gynt" and still held
the yokelry agape.   The same talent, raised to a high
power, is in this Prof. Dr. Veblen.   Tunnel under his
great moraines and stalagmites of words, dig down
into his vast kitchen-midden of discordant and raucous polysyllables, blow up the hard, thick shell of
his almost theological manner, and what you will find
in his discourse is chiefly a mass of platitudes—the
self-evident made horrifying, the obvious in terms of
the staggering.   Marx, I daresay, said a good deal of
it, and what Marx overlooked has been said over and
over again by his heirs and assigns.   But Marx, at
this business, labored under a technical handicap: he
wrote in German, a language he actually understood.
Prof. Dr. Veblen submits himself to no such disad-
vantage.   Though born, I believe, in These States,
and resident here all his life, he achieves the effect,

perhaps without employing the means, of thinking in some unearthly foreign language—say Swahili, Sumerian or Old Bulgarian—and then painfully clawing his thoughts into a copious but uncertain and book-learned English. The result is a style that affects the higher cerebral centers like a constant roll of subway expresses. The second result is a sort of bewildered numbness of the senses, as before some fabulous and unearthly marvel. And the third result, if I make no mistake, is the celebrity of the professor as a Great Thinker. In brief, he states his hollow nothings in such high, astounding terms that they must inevitably arrest and blister the right-thinking mind. He makes them mysterious. He makes them shocking. He makes them portentous. And so, flinging them at naïve and believing minds, he makes them stick and burn.

No doubt you think that I exaggerate—perhaps even that I lie. If so, then consider this specimen—the first paragraph of Chapter XIII of "The Theory of the Leisure Class":

In an increasing proportion as time goes on, the anthropomorphic cult, with its code of devout observances, suffers a progressive disintegration through the stress of economic exigencies and the decay of the system of status. As this disintegration proceeds, there come to be associated and blended with the devout attitude certain other motives and impulses that are not always of an anthropomorphic origin, nor traceable to the habit of personal subservience.

Not all of these subsidiary impulses that blend with the bait of devoutness in the later devotional life are altogether congruous with the devout attitude or with the anthropomorphic apprehension of sequence of phenomena. Their origin being not the same, their action upon the scheme of devout life is also not in the same direction. In many ways they traverse the underlying norm of subservience or vicarious life to which the code of devout observances and the ecclesiastical and sacerdotal institutions are to be traced as their substantial basis. Through the presence of these alien motives the social and industrial régime of status gradually disintegrates, and the canon of personal subservience loses the support derived from an unbroken tradition. Extraneous habits and proclivities encroach upon the field of action occupied by this canon, and it presently comes about that the ecclesiastical and sacerdotal structures are partially converted to other uses, in some measure alien to the purposes of the scheme of devout life as it stood in the days of the most vigorous and characteristic development of the priesthood.

Well, what have we here? What does this appalling salvo of rhetorical artillery signify? What is the sweating professor trying to say? What is his Message now? Simply that in the course of time, the worship of God is commonly corrupted by other enterprises, and that the church, ceasing to be a mere temple of adoration, becomes the headquarters of these other enterprises. More simply still, that men sometimes vary serving God by serving other men, which means, of course, serving themselves. This

bald platitude, which must be obvious to any child
who has ever been to a church bazaar or a parish
house, is here tortured, worried and run through roll-
ers until it is spread out to 241 words, of which fully
200 are unnecessary. The next paragraph is even
worse. In it the master undertakes to explain in
his peculiar dialect the meaning of "that non-reverent
sense of æsthetic congruity with the environment
which is left as a residue of the latter-day act of worship after elimination of its anthropomorphic content." Just what does he mean by this "non-reverent
sense of æsthetic congruity"? I have studied the
whole paragraph for three days, halting only for
prayer and sleep, and I have come to certain conclusions. I may be wrong, but nevertheless it is the best
that I can do. What I conclude is this: he is trying
to say that many people go to church, not because
they are afraid of the devil but because they enjoy
the music, and like to look at the stained glass, the
potted lilies and the rev. pastor. To get this profound and highly original observation upon paper,
he wastes, not merely 241, but more than 300 words!
To say what might be said on a postage stamp he
takes more than a page in his book! . . .

And so it goes, alas, alas, in all his other volumes
—a cent's worth of information wrapped in a bale of
polysyllables. In "The Higher Learning in America" the thing perhaps reaches its damndest and worst.

It is as if the practice of that incredibly obscure and malodorous style were a relentless disease, a sort of progressive intellectual diabetes, a leprosy of the horse sense. Words are flung upon words until all recollection that there must be a meaning in them, a ground and excuse for them, is lost. One wanders in a labyrinth of nouns, adjectives, verbs, pronouns, adverbs, prepositions, conjunctions and participles, most of them swollen and nearly all of them unable to walk. It is difficult to imagine worse English, within the limits of intelligible grammar. It is clumsy, affected, opaque, bombastic, windy, empty. It is without grace or distinction and it is often without the most elementary order. The learned professor gets himself enmeshed in his gnarled sentences like a bull trapped by barbed wire, and his efforts to extricate himself are quite as furious and quite as spectacular. He heaves, he leaps, he writhes; at times he seems to be at the point of yelling for the police. It is a picture to bemuse the vulgar and to give the judicious grief.

Worse, there is nothing at the bottom of all this strident wind-music—the ideas it is designed to set forth are, in the overwhelming main, poor ideas, and often they are ideas that are almost idiotic. One never gets the thrill of sharp and original thinking, dexterously put into phrases. The concepts underlying, say, "The Theory of the Leisure Class" are simply Socialism and water; the concepts underlying "The Higher Learning in America" are so childishly obvious that even the poor drudges who write editorials for newspapers have often voiced them. When, now and then, the professor tires of this emission of stale bosh and attempts flights of a more original character, he straightway comes tumbling down into absurdity. What the reader then has to struggle with is not only intolerably bad writing, but also loose, flabby, cocksure and preposterous thinking. . . . Again I take refuge in an example. It is from Chapter IV of "The Theory of the Leisure Class." The problem before the author here has to do with the social convention which frowns upon the consumption of alcohol by women—at least to the extent to which men may consume it decorously. Well, then, what is his explanation of this convention? Here, in brief, is his process of reasoning:

1. The leisure class, which is the predatory class of feudal times, reserves all luxuries for itself, and disapproves their use by members of the lower classes, for this use takes away their charm by taking away their exclusive possession.

2. Women are chattels in the possession of the leisure class, and hence subject to the rules made for inferiors. "The patriarchal tradition . . . says that the woman, being a chattel, should consume only what is necessary to her sustenance, except so far as her further consumption contributes to the comfort or the good repute of her master."

3. The consumption of alcohol contributes nothing to the comfort or good repute of the woman's master, but "detracts sensibly from the comfort or pleasure" of her master. *Ergo,* she is forbidden to drink.

This, I believe, is a fair specimen of the Veblenian ratiocination. Observe it well, for it is typical. That is to say, it starts off with a gratuitous and highly dubious assumption, proceeds to an equally dubious deduction, and then ends with a platitude which begs the whole question. What sound reason is there for believing that exclusive possession is the hall-mark of luxury? There is none that I can see. It may be true of a few luxuries, but it is certainly not true of the most familiar ones. Do I enjoy a decent bath because I know that John Smith cannot afford one —or because I delight in being clean? Do I admire Beethoven's Fifth Symphony because it is incomprehensible to Congressmen and Methodists—or because I genuinely love music? Do I prefer terrapin à la Maryland to fried liver because plowhands must put up with the liver—or because the terrapin is intrinsically a more charming dose? Do I prefer kissing a pretty girl to kissing a charwoman because even a janitor may kiss a charwoman—or because the pretty girl looks better, smells better and kisses better? Now and then, to be sure, the idea of exclusive possession enters into the concept of luxury. I may, if I am a bibliophile, esteem a book because it is a unique first edition. I may, if I am fond, esteem a woman because she smiles on no one else. But even here, save in a very small minority of cases, other attractions plainly enter into the matter. It pleases me to have a unique first edition, but I wouldn't care anything for a unique first edition of Robert W. Chambers or Elinor Glyn; the author must have my respect, the book must be intrinsically valuable, there must be much more to it than its mere uniqueness. And if, being fond, I glory in the exclusive smiles of a certain Miss —— or Mrs. ——, then surely my satisfaction depends chiefly upon the lady herself, and not upon my mere monopoly. Would I delight in the fidelity of the charwoman? Would it give me any joy to learn that, through a sense of duty to me, she had ceased to kiss the janitor?

Confronted by such considerations, it seems to me that there is little truth left in Prof. Dr. Veblen's theory of conspicuous consumption and conspicuous waste—that what remains of it, after it is practically applied a few times, is no more than a wraith of balderdash. In so far as it is true it is obvious. All the professor accomplishes with it is to take what every one knows and pump it up to such proportions that every one begins to doubt it. What could be plainer than his failure in the case just cited? He starts off with a platitude, and ends in absurdity. No one denies, I take it, that in a clearly limited sense,

women occupy a place in the world—or, more accurately, aspire to a place in the world—that is a
good deal like that of a chattel.   Marriage, the goal
of their only honest and permanent hopes, invades
their individuality; a married woman becomes the
function of another individuality.   Thus the appearance she presents to the world is often the mirror of
her husband's egoism.   A rich man hangs his wife
with expensive clothes and jewels for the same reason,
among others, that he adorns his own head with a
plug hat: to notify everybody that he can afford it
—in brief, to excite the envy of Socialists.   But he
also does it, let us hope, for another and far better
and more powerful reason, to wit, that she intrigues
him, that he delights in her, that he loves her—and
so wants to make her gaudy and happy.   This reason
may not appeal to Socialist sociologists.   In Russia,
according to an old scandal (officially endorsed by
the British bureau for pulling Yankee noses) the
Bolsheviki actually repudiated it as insane.   Nevertheless, it continues to appeal very forcibly to the
majority of normal husbands in the nations of the
West, and I am convinced that it is a hundred times
as potent as any other reason.   The American husband, in particular, dresses his wife like a circus
horse, not primarily because he wants to display his
wealth upon her person, but because he is a soft and
moony fellow and ever ready to yield to her desires,

however preposterous. If any conception of her as
a chattel were actively in him, even unconsciously, he
would be a good deal less her slave. As it is, her
vicarious practice of conspicuous waste commonly
reaches such a development that her master himself
is forced into renunciations—which brings Prof. Dr.
Veblen's theory to self-destruction.

His final conclusion is as unsound as his premisses.
All it comes to is a plain begging of the question.
Why does a man forbid his wife to drink all the alcohol she can hold? Because, he says, it "detracts
sensibly from his comfort or pleasure." In other
words, it detracts from his comfort and pleasure because it detracts from his comfort and pleasure.
Meanwhile, the real answer is so plain that even a
professor should know it. A man forbids his wife
to drink too much because, deep in his secret archives,
he has records of the behavior of other women who
drank too much, and is eager to safeguard his wife's
self-respect and his own dignity against what he
knows to be certain invasion. In brief, it is a commonplace of observation, familiar to all males beyond the age of twenty-one, that once a woman is
drunk the rest is a mere matter of time and place:
the girl is already there. A husband, viewing this
prospect, perhaps shrinks from having his chattel
damaged. But let us be soft enough to think that he
may also shrink from seeing humiliation, ridicule and

bitter regret inflicted upon one who is under his protection, and one whose dignity and happiness are
precious to him, and one whom he regards with deep
and (I surely hope) lasting affection. A man's
grandfather is surely not his chattel, even by the
terms of the Veblen theory, and yet I am sure that no
sane man would let the old gentleman go beyond a dis-
creet cocktail or two if a bout of genuine bibbing were
certain to be followed by the complete destruction of
his dignity, his chastity and (if a Presbyterian) his
immortal soul. . . .

One more example of the Veblenian logic and I
must pass on: I have other fish to fry. On page
135 of "The Theory of the Leisure Class" he turns
his garish and buzzing search-light upon another
problem of the domestic hearth, this time a double
one. First, why do we have lawns around our country houses? Secondly, why don't we employ cows to
keep them clipped, instead of importing Italians,
Croatians and blackamoors? The first question is
answered by an appeal to ethnology: we delight in
lawns because we are the descendants of "a pastoral
people inhabiting a region with a humid climate."
True enough, there is in a well-kept lawn "an element
of sensuous beauty," but that is secondary: the main
thing is that our dolicho-blond ancestors had flocks,
and thus took a keen professional interest in grass.
(The Marx *motif!* The economic interpretation of

history in E flat.) But why don't *we* keep flocks? Why do we renounce cows and hire Jugo-Slavs? Because "to the average popular apprehension a herd of cattle so pointedly suggests thrift and usefulness that their presence . . . would be intolerably cheap." With the highest veneration, Bosh! Plowing through a bad book from end to end, I can find nothing sillier than this. Here, indeed, the whole "theory of conspicuous waste" is exposed for precisely what it is: one per cent. platitude and ninety-nine per cent. nonsense. Has the genial professor, pondering his great problems, ever taken a walk in the country? And has he, in the course of that walk, ever crossed a pasture inhabited by a cow (*Bos taurus*)? And has he, making that crossing, ever passed astern of the cow herself? And has he, thus passing astern, ever stepped carelessly, and—

But this is not a medical work, and so I had better haul up. The cow, to me, symbolizes the whole speculation of this laborious and humorless pedagogue. From end to end you will find the same tedious torturing of plain facts, the same relentless piling up of thin and over-labored theory, the same flatulent bombast, the same intellectual strabismus. And always with an air of vast importance, always in vexed and formidable sentences, always in the longest words possible, always in the most cacophonous English that even a professor ever wrote. One visualizes him with his head thrown back, searching for cryptic answers in the firmament and not seeing the overt and disconcerting cow, not watching his step. One sees him as the pundit *par excellence,* infinitely earnest and diligent, infinitely honest and patient, but also infinitely humorless, futile and hollow. . . .

So much, at least for the present, for this Prof. Dr. Thorstein Veblen, head Great Thinker to the parlor radicals, Socrates of the intellectual Greenwich Village, chief star (at least transiently) of the American *Athanœums.* I am tempted to crowd in mention of some of his other astounding theories—for example, the theory that the presence of pupils, the labor of teaching, a concern with pedagogy, is necessary to the highest functioning of a scientific investigator— a notion magnificently supported by the examples of Flexner, Ehrlich, Metchnikoff, Loeb and Carrel! I am tempted, too, to devote a thirdly to the astounding materialism, almost the downright hoggishness, of his whole system—its absolute exclusion of everything approaching an æsthetic motive. But I must leave all these fallacies and absurdities to your own inquiry. More important than any of them, more important as a phenomenon than the professor himself and all his works, is the gravity with which his muddled and highly dubious ideas have been received. At the moment, I daresay, he is in decline; such Great Thinkers have a way of going out as quickly as they come in. But a year or so ago he dominated the American scene. All the reviews were full of his ideas. A hundred lesser sages reflected them. Every one of intellectual pretentions read his books. Veblenism was shining in full brilliance. There were Veblenists, Veblen clubs, Veblen remedies for all the sorrows of the world. There were even, in Chicago, Veblen Girls—perhaps Gibson girls grown middle-aged and despairing.

The spectacle, unluckily, was not novel. Go back through the history of America since the early nineties, and you will find a long succession of just such violent and uncritical enthusiasms. James had his day; Dewey had his day; Ibsen had his day; Maeterlinck had his day. Almost every year sees another intellectual Munyon arise, with his infallible peruna for all the current malaises. Sometimes this Great Thinker is imported. Once he was Pastor Wagner; once he was Bergson; once he was Eucken; once he was Tolstoi; once he was a lady, by name Ellen Key; again he was another lady, Signorina Montessori. But more often he is of native growth, and full of the pervasive cocksureness and superficiality of the land. I do not rank Dr. Veblen among the worst of these haruspices, save perhaps as a stylist; I am actually convinced that he belongs among the best of them. But that best is surely depressing enough. What lies behind it is the besetting intellectual sin of

the United States—the habit of turning intellectual
concepts into emotional concepts, the vice of orgiastic
and inflammatory thinking. There is, in America,
no orderly and thorough working out of the fundamental problems of our society; there is only, as one
Englishman has said, an eternal combat of crazes.
The things of capital importance are habitually discussed, not by men soberly trying to get at the truth
about them, but by brummagem Great Thinkers trying only to get *kudos* out of them. We are beset endlessly by quacks—and they are not the less quacks
when they happen to be quite honest. In all fields,
from politics to pedagogics and from theology to public hygiene, there is a constant emotional obscuration
of the true issues, a violent combat of credulities, an
inane debasement of scientific curiosity to the level
of mob gaping.

The thing to blame, of course, is our lack of an intellectual aristocracy—sound in its information, skep-
tical in its habit of mind, and, above all, secure in
its position and authority. Every other civilized
country has such an aristocracy. It is the natural
corrective of enthusiasms from below. It is hospitable to ideas, but as adamant against crazes. It
stands against the pollution of logic by emotion, the
sophistication of evidence to the glory of God. But in
America there is nothing of the sort. On the one
hand there is the populace—perhaps more powerful

here, more capable of putting its idiotic ideas into execution, than anywhere else—and surely more eager to
follow platitudinous messiahs. On the other hand
there is the ruling plutocracy—ignorant, hostile to
inquiry, tyrannical in the exercise of its power, suspicious of ideas of whatever sort. In the middle
ground there is little save an indistinct herd of intellectual eunuchs, chiefly professors—often quite as
stupid as the plutocracy and always in great fear of
it. When it produces a stray rebel he goes over to
the mob; there is no place for him within his own
order. This feeble and vacillating class, unorgan-
ized and without authority, is responsible for what
passes as the well-informed opinion of the country—
for the sort of opinion that one encounters in the serious periodicals—for what later on leaks down, much
diluted, into the few newspapers that are not frankly
imbecile. Dr. Veblen has himself described it in
"The Higher Learning in America"; he is one of its
characteristic products, and he proves that he is thoroughly of it by the timorousness he shows in that book.
It is, in the main, only half-educated. It lacks experience of the world, assurance, the consciousness of
class solidarity and security. Of no definite position
in our national life, exposed alike to the clamors of
the mob and the discipline of the plutocracy, it gets no
public respect and is deficient in self-respect. Thus
the better sort of men are not tempted to enter it. It

recruits only men of feeble courage, men of small originality. Its sublimest flower is the American college president, well described by Dr. Veblen—a perambulating sycophant and platitudinarian, a gaudy mendicant and bounder, engaged all his life, not in the battle of ideas, the pursuit and dissemination of knowledge, but in the courting of rich donkeys and the entertainment of mobs. . . .

Nay, Veblen is not the worst.   Veblen is almost the best.   The worst is—but I begin to grow indignant, and indignation, as old Friedrich used to say, is foreign to my nature.

VI. THE NEW POETRY
MOVEMENT

THE current pother about poetry, now gradually subsiding, seems to have begun about seven years ago—say in 1912. It was during that year that Harriet Monroe established *Poetry: A Magazine of Verse,* in Chicago, and ever since then she has been the mother superior of the movement. Other leaders have occasionally disputed her command—the bombastic Braithwaite, with his annual anthology of magazine verse; Amy Lowell, with her solemn pronunciamentos in the manner of a Harvard professor; Vachel Lindsay, with his nebulous vaporings and chautauqua posturings; even such cheap jacks as Alfred Kreymborg, out of Greenwich Village. But the importance of Miss Monroe grows more manifest as year chases year. She was, to begin with, clearly the pioneer. *Poetry* was on the stands nearly two years before the first Braithwaite anthology, and long before Miss Lowell had been lured from her earlier finishing-school doggerels by the Franco-British Imagists. It antedated, too, all the other salient documents of the movement—Master's "Spoon River

Anthology," Frost's "North of Boston," Lindsay's
"General William Booth Enters Heaven," the historic
bulls of the Imagists, the frantic balderdash of the
"Others" group.   Moreover, Miss Monroe has always
managed to keep on good terms with all wings of the
heaven-kissed host, and has thus managed to exert
a ponderable influence both to starboard and to port.
This, I daresay, is because she is a very intelligent
woman, which fact is alone sufficient to give her an
austere   eminence   in   a   movement   so   beset   by
mountebanks and their dupes.   I have read *Poetry*
since the first number, and find it constantly entertaining.   It has printed a great deal of extravagant stuff,
and not a little downright nonsensical stuff, but in the
main it has steered a safe and intelligible course,
with no salient blunders.   No other poetry magazine
—and there have been dozens of them—has even remotely approached it in interest, or, for that matter,
in genuine hospitality to ideas.   Practically all of
the others have been operated by passionate enthusiasts, often extremely ignorant and always narrow and
humorless.   But Miss Monroe has managed to retain
a certain judicial calm in the midst of all the whooping and clapper-clawing, and so she has avoided running amuck, and her magazine has printed the very
best of the new poetry and avoided much of the worst.

As I say, the movement shows signs of having spent
its strength.   The mere bulk of the verse that it pro-

duces is a great deal less than it was three or four
years ago, or even one or two years ago, and there is
a noticeable tendency toward the conservatism once
so loftily disdained. I daresay the Knish-Morgan
burlesque of Witter Bynner and Arthur Davison Ficke
was a hard blow to the more fantastic radicals. At
all events, they subsided after it was perpetrated, and
for a couple of years nothing has been heard from
them. These radicals, chiefly collected in what was
called the "Others" group, rattled the slapstick in a
sort of side-show to the main exhibition. They at-
tracted, of course, all the more credulous and unin-
formed partisans of the movement, and not a few ad-
vanced professors out of one-building universities began to lecture upon them before bucolic women's
clubs. They committed hari-kari in the end by beginning to believe in their own buncombe. When
their leaders took to the chautauquas and sought to
convince the peasantry that James Whitcomb Riley
was a fraud the time was ripe for the lethal buffoonery
of MM. Bynner and Ficke. That buffoonery was
enormously successful—perhaps the best hoax in
American literary history. It was swallowed, indeed,
by so many magnificoes that it made criticism very
timorous thereafter, and so did damage to not a few
quite honest bards. To-day a new poet, if he departs ever so little from the path already beaten, is
kept in a sort of literary delousing pen until it is

established that he is genuinely sincere, and not merely another Bynner in hempen whiskers and a cloak to go invisible.

Well, what is the net produce of the whole uproar? How much actual poetry have all these truculent rebels against Stedman's Anthology and McGuffey's Sixth Reader manufactured? I suppose I have read nearly all of it—a great deal of it, as a magazine editor, in manuscript—and yet, as I look back, my memory is lighted up by very few flashes of any lasting brilliance. The best of all the lutists of the new school, I am inclined to think, are Carl Sandburg and James Oppenheim, and particularly Sandburg. He shows a great deal of raucous crudity, he is often a bit uncertain and wobbly, and sometimes he is downright banal—but, taking one bard with another, he is probably the soundest and most intriguing of the lot. Compare, for example, his war poems—simple, eloquent and extraordinarily moving—to the humorless balderdash of Amy Lowell, or, to go outside the movement, to the childish gush of Joyce Kilmer, Hermann Hagedorn and Charles Hanson Towne. Often he gets memorable effects by astonishingly austere means, as in his famous "Chicago" rhapsody and his "Cool Tombs." And always he is thoroughly individual, a true original, his own man. Oppenheim, equally eloquent, is more conventional. He stands, as to one leg, on the shoulders of Walt Whitman, and,

as to the other, on a stack of Old Testaments. The
stuff he writes, despite his belief to the contrary, is
not American at all; it is absolutely Jewish, Levantine, almost Asiatic. But here is something criticism
too often forgets: the Jew, intrinsically, is the greatest
of poets. Beside his gorgeous rhapsodies the highest flights of any western bard seem feeble and cerebral. Oppenheim, inhabiting a brick house in New
York, manages to get that sonorous Eastern note into
his dithyrambs. They are often inchoate and fever-
ish, but at their best they have the gigantic gusto of
Solomon's Song.

Miss Lowell is the schoolmarm of the movement,
and vastly more the pedagogue than the artist. She
has written perhaps half a dozen excellent pieces in
imitation of Richard Aldington and John Gould
Fletcher, and a great deal of highfalutin bathos.
Her "A Dome of Many-Colored Glass" is full of infantile poppycock, and though it is true that it was
first printed in 1912, before she joined the Imagists,
it is not to be forgotten that it was reprinted with her
consent in 1915, after she had definitely set up shop
as a foe of the *cliché*. Her celebrity, I fancy, is
largely extra-poetical; if she were Miss Tilly Jones,
of Fort Smith, Ark., there would be a great deal less
rowing about her, and her successive masterpieces
would be received less gravely. A literary craftsman in America, as I have already said once or twice,

is never judged by his work alone. Miss Lowell has
been helped very much by her excellent social position. The majority, and perhaps fully nine-tenths
of the revolutionary poets are of no social position at
all—newspaper reporters, Jews, foreigners of vague
nationality, school teachers, lawyers, advertisement
writers, itinerant lecturers, Greenwich Village pos-
turers, and so on. I have a suspicion that it has
subtly flattered such denizens of the *demi-monde* to
find the sister of a president of Harvard in their midst,
and that their delight has materially corrupted their
faculties. Miss Lowell's book of exposition, "Tendencies in Modern American Poetry," is commonplace to the last degree. Louis Untermeyer's "The
New Era in American Poetry" is very much better.
And so is Prof. Dr. John Livingston Lowes' "Convention and Revolt in Poetry."

As for Edgar Lee Masters, for a short season the
undisputed Homer of the movement, I believe that he
is already extinct. What made the fame of "The
Spoon River Anthology" was not chiefly any great
show of novelty in it, nor any extraordinary poign-
ancy, nor any grim truthfulness unparalleled, but
simply the public notion that it was improper. It
fell upon the country at the height of the last sex
wave—a wave eternally ebbing and flowing, now high,
now low. It was read, not as work of art, but as
document; its large circulation was undoubtedly

mainly among persons to whom poetry *qua* poetry was as sour a dose as symphonic music. To such persons, of course, it seemed something new under the sun. They were unacquainted with the verse of George Crabbe; they were quite innocent of E. A. Robinson and Robert Frost; they knew nothing of the *Ubi sunt* formula; they had never heard of the Greek Anthology. The roar of his popular success won Masters' case with the critics. His undoubted merits in detail—his half-wistful cynicism, his capacity for evoking simple emotions, his deft skill at managing the puny difficulties of *vers libre*—were thereupon pumped up to such an extent that his defects were lost sight of. Those defects, however, shine blindingly in his later books. Without the advantage of content that went with the anthology, they reveal themselves as volumes of empty doggerel, with now and then a brief moment of illumination. It would be difficult, indeed, to find poetry that is, in essence, less poetical. Most of the pieces are actually tracts, and many of them are very bad tracts.

Lindsay? Alas, he has done his own burlesque. What was new in him, at the start, was an echo of the barbaric rhythms of the Jubilee Songs. But very soon the thing ceased to be a marvel, and of late his elephantine college yells have ceased to be amusing. His retirement to the chautauquas is self-criticism of uncommon penetration. Frost? A standard New

England poet, with a few changes in phraseology, and
the substitution of sour resignationism for sweet resignationism. Whittier without the whiskers. Robinson? Ditto, but with a politer bow. He has written
sound poetry, but not much of it. The late Major-
General Roosevelt ruined him by praising him, as he
ruined Henry Bordeaux, Pastor Wagner, Francis War-
rington Dawson and many another. Giovannitti?
A forth-rate Sandburg. Ezra Pound? The American in headlong flight from America—to England, to
Italy, to the Middle Ages, to ancient Greece, to Cathay
and points East. Pound, it seems to me, is the most
picturesque man in the whole movement—a professor
turned fantee, Abelard in grand opera. His knowledge is abysmal; he has it readily on tap; moreover,
he has a fine ear, and has written many an excellent
verse. But now all the glow and gusto of the bard
have been transformed into the rage of the pam-
phleteer: he drops the lute for the bayonet. One
sympathizes with him in his choler. The stupidity he
combats is actually almost unbearable. Every
normal man must be tempted, at times, to spit on his
hands, hoist the black flag, and begin slitting throats.
But this business, alas, is fatal to the placid moods
and fine other-worldliness of the poet. Pound gives a
thrilling show, but—. . . . The remaining stars of
the liberation need not detain us. They are the street-
boys following the calliope. They have labored with

diligence, but they have produced no poetry. . . .

Miss Monroe, if she would write a book about it, would be the most competent historian of the movement, and perhaps also its keenest critic. She has seen it from the inside. She knows precisely what it is about. She is able, finally, to detach herself from its extravagances, and to estimate its opponents without bile. Her failure to do a volume about it leaves Untermeyer's "The New Era in American Poetry" the best in the field. Prof. Dr. Lowes' treatise is very much more thorough, but it has the defect of stopping with the fundamentals—it has too little to say about specific poets. Untermeyer discusses all of them, and then throws in a dozen or two orthodox bards, wholly untouched by Bolshevism, for good measure. His criticism is often trenchant and always very clear. He thinks he knows what he thinks he knows, and he states it with the utmost address— sometimes, indeed, as in the case of Pound, with a good deal more address than its essential accuracy deserves. But the messianic note that gets into the bulls and ukases of Pound himself, the profound solemnity of Miss Lowell, the windy chautauqua-like nothings of Lindsay, the contradictions of the Imagists, the puerilities of Kreymborg *et al*—all these things are happily absent. And so it is possible to follow him amiably even when he is palpably wrong.

That is not seldom. At the very start, for example,

he permits himself a lot of highly dubious rumble-
bumble about the "inherent Americanism" and soaring democracy of the movement. "Once," he says,
"the most exclusive and aristocratic of the arts, ap-
preciated and fostered only by little *salons* and eru-
dite groups, poetry has suddenly swung away from
its self-imposed strictures and is expressing itself once
more in terms of democracy." Pondering exces-
sively, I can think of nothing that would be more untrue than this. The fact is that the new poetry is
neither American nor democratic. Despite its remote grounding on Whitman, it started, not in the
United States at all, but in France, and its exotic
color is still its most salient characteristic. Practically every one of its practitioners is palpably under some strong foreign influence, and most of them
are no more Anglo-Saxon than a samovar or a toccata.
The deliberate strangeness of Pound, his almost
fanatical anti-Americanism, is a mere accentuation
of what is in every other member of the fraternity.
Many of them, like Frost, Fletcher, H. D. and Pound,
have exiled themselves from the republic. Others,
such as Oppenheim, Sandburg, Giovannitti, Benét and
Untermeyer himself, are palpably Continental Euro-
peans, often with Levantine traces. Yet others, such
as Miss Lowell and Masters, are little more, at their
best, than translators and adapters—from the French,
from the Japanese, from the Greek. Even Lindsay,

superficially the most national of them all, has also his exotic smear, as I have shown. Let Miss Lowell herself be a witness. "We shall see them," she says at the opening of her essay on E. A. Robinson, "ceding more and more to the influence of other, alien, peoples. . . ." A glance is sufficient to show the correctness of this observation. There is no more "inherent Americanism" in the new poetry than there is in the new American painting and music. It lies, in fact, quite outside the main stream of American culture.

Nor is it democratic, in any intelligible sense. The poetry of Whittier and Longfellow was democratic. It voiced the elemental emotions of the masses of the people; it was full of their simple, rubber-stamp ideas; they comprehended it and cherished it. And so with the poetry of James Whitcomb Riley, and with that of Walt Mason and Ella Wheeler Wilcox. But the new poetry, grounded firmly upon novelty of form and boldness of idea, is quite beyond their understanding. It seems to them to be idiotic, just as the poetry of Whitman seemed to them to be idiotic, and if they could summon up enough interest in it to examine it at length they would undoubtedly clamor for laws making the confection of it a felony. The mistake of Untermeyer, and of others who talk to the same effect, lies in confusing the beliefs of poets and the subject matter of their verse with its position in

the national consciousness. Oppenheim, Sandburg
and Lindsay are democrats, just as Whitman was a
democrat, but their poetry is no more a democratic
phenomenon than his was, or than, to go to music,
Beethoven's Eroica Symphony was. Many of the
new poets, in truth, are ardent enemies of democracy,
for example, Pound. Only one of them has ever
actually sought to take his strophes to the vulgar.
That one is Lindsay—and there is not the slightest
doubt that the yokels welcomed him, not because they
were interested in his poetry, but because it struck
them as an amazing, and perhaps even a fascinatingly
obscene thing, for a sane man to go about the country
on any such bizarre and undemocratic business.

No sound art, in fact, could possibly be democratic.
Tolstoi wrote a whole book to prove the contrary, and
only succeeded in making his case absurd.   The only
art that is capable of reaching the *Homo Boobus* is
art that is already debased and polluted—band music,
official sculpture, Pears' Soap painting, the popular
novel.   What is honest and worthy of praise in the
new poetry is Greek to the general.   And, despite
much nonsense, it seems to me that there is no little
in it that is honest and worthy of praise.   It has, for
one thing, made an effective war upon the *cliché*, and
so purged the verse of the nation of much of its old
banality in subject and phrase.   The elegant album
pieces of Richard Henry Stoddard and Edmund Clar-

ence Stedman are no longer in fashion—save, perhaps, among the democrats that Untermeyer mentions.
And in the second place, it has substituted for this ancient conventionality an eager curiosity in life as men
and women are actually living it—a spirit of daring
experimentation that has made poetry vivid and full
of human interest, as it was in the days of Elizabeth.
The thing often passes into the grotesque, it is shot
through and through with *héliogabalisme,* but at its
high points it has achieved invaluable pioneering.   A
new poet, emerging out of the Baptist night of Peoria
or Little Rock to-day, comes into an atmosphere
charged with subtle electricities.   There is a stimulating restlessness; ideas have a welcome; the art he
aspires to is no longer a merely formal exercise, like
practicing Czerny.   When a Henry Van Dyke arises
at some college banquet and begins to discharge an
old-fashioned ode to *alma mater* there is a definite
snicker; it is almost as if he were to appear in Congress gaiters or a beaver hat.   An audience for such
things, of course, still exists.   It is, no doubt, an
enormously large audience.   But it has changed a
good deal qualitatively, if not quantitatively.   The
relatively civilized reader has been educated to something better.   He has heard a music that has spoiled
his ear for the old wheezing of the melodeon.   He
weeps no more over what wrung him yesteryear.

Unluckily, the new movement, in America even

more than in England, France and Germany, suffers from a very crippling lack, and that is the lack of a genuinely first-rate poet. It has produced many talents, but it has yet to produce any genius, or even the shadow of genius. There has been a general lifting of the plain, but no vasty and melodramatic throwing up of new peaks. Worse still, it has had to face hard competition from without—that is, from poets who, while also emerged from platitude, have yet stood outside it, and perhaps in some doubt of it. Untermeyer discusses a number of such poets in his book. There is one of them, Lizette Woodworth Reese, who has written more sound poetry, more genuinely eloquent and beautiful poetry, than all the new poets put together—more than a whole posse of Masterses and Lindsays, more than a hundred Amy Lowells. And there are others, Neihardt and John McClure among them—particularly McClure. Untermeyer, usually anything but an ass, once committed the unforgettable asininity of sneering at McClure. The blunder, I daresay, is already lamented; it is not embalmed in his book. But it will haunt him on Tyburn Hill. For this McClure, attempting the simplest thing in the simplest way, has done it almost superbly. He seems to be entirely without theories. There is no pedagogical passion in him. He is no reformer. But more than any of the reformers now or lately in the arena, he is a poet.

VII. THE HEIR OF MARK TWAIN

NOTHING could be stranger than the current celebrity of Irvin S. Cobb, an author of whom almost as much is heard as if he were a new Thackeray or Molière. One is solemnly told by various extravagant partisans, some of them not otherwise insane, that he is at once the successor to Mark Twain and the heir of Edgar Allan Poe. One hears of public dinners given in devotion to his genius, of public presentations, of learned degrees conferred upon him by universities, of other extraordinary adulations, few of them shared by such relatively puny fellows as Howells and Dreiser. His talents and sagacity pass into popular anecdotes; he has sedulous Boswells; he begins to take on the august importance of an actor-manager. Behind the scenes, of course, a highly dexterous publisher pulls the strings, but much of it is undoubtedly more or less sincere; men pledge their sacred honor to the doctrine that his existence honors the national literature. Moreover, he seems to take the thing somewhat seriously himself. He gives his *imprimatur* to various other authors, including Joseph Conrad; he engages himself to lift the literary tone of moving-pictures; he lends his name to movements; he exposes himself in the chautauquas; he takes on the responsibilities of a patriot and a public man. . . . Altogether, a curious, and, in some of its aspects, a caressingly ironical spectacle. One wonders what the graduate sophomores of to-morrow, composing their dull tomes upon American letters, will make of it. . . .

In the actual books of the man I can find nothing that seems to justify so much enthusiasm, nor even the hundredth part of it. His serious fiction shows a certain undoubted facility, but there are at least forty other Americans who do the thing quite as well. His public bulls and ukases are no more than clever journalism—superficial and inconsequential, first saying one thing and then quite another thing. And in his humor, which his admirers apparently put first among his products, I can discover, at best, nothing save a somewhat familiar aptitude for grotesque anecdote, and, at worst, only the laborious laugh-squeezing of Bill Nye. In the volume called "Those Times and These" there is an excellent comic story, to wit, "Hark, From the Tomb!" But it would surely be an imbecility to call it a masterpiece; too many other authors have done things quite as good; more than a few (I need cite only George Ade, Owen Johnson and Ring W. Lardner) have done things very much better. Worse, it lies in the book like a slice of Smithfield ham between two slabs of stale store-bread. On both sides of it are very stupid artificialities—stories without point, stories in which rustic characters try to talk like Wilson Mizner, stories altogether machine-made and depressing. Turn, now, to another book, vastly praised in its year—by name, "Cobb's Anatomy." One laughs occasionally— but precisely as one laughs over a comic supplement or the jokes in *Ayer's Almanac.* For example:

> There never was a hansom cab made that would hold a fat man comfortably unless he left the doors open, and that makes him feel undressed.

Again:

> Your hair gives you bother so long as you have it and more bother when it starts to go. You are always doing something for it and it is always showing deep-dyed ingratitude in return; or else the dye isn't deep enough, which is even worse.

Exactly; it is even worse. And then this:

> Once there was a manicure lady who wouldn't take a tip, but she is now no more. Her indignant sisters stabbed her to death with hatpins and nail-files.

I do not think I quote unfairly; I have tried to select honest specimens of the author's fancy. . . . Perhaps it may be well to glance at another book. I choose, at random, "Speaking of Operations—," a

work described by the publisher as "the funniest yet
written by Cobb" and "the funniest book we know of."
In this judgment many other persons seem to have
concurred. The thing was an undoubted success when
it appeared as an article in the *Saturday Evening Post*
and it sold thousands of copies between covers.
Well, what is in it? In it, after a diligent reading,
I find half a dozen mildly clever observations—and
sixty odd pages of ancient and infantile wheezes, as
flat to the taste as so many crystals of hyposulphite of
soda. For example, the wheeze to the effect that in
the days of the author's nonage "germs had not been
invented yet." For example, the wheeze to the effect
that doctors bury their mistakes. For example, the
wheeze to the effect that the old-time doctor always
prescribed medicines of abominably evil flavor. . . .
But let us go into the volume more in detail, and so
unearth all its gems.

On page 1, in the very first paragraph, there is the
doddering old joke about the steepness of doctors'
bills. In the second paragraph there is the somewhat
newer but still fully adult joke about the extreme
willingness of persons who have been butchered by
surgeons to talk about it afterward. These two wit-
ticisms are all that I can find on page 1. For the rest,
it consists almost entirely of a reference to MM. Bryan
and Roosevelt—a reference well known by all newspaper paragraphists and vaudeville monologists to

be as provocative of laughter as a mention of bunions, mothers-in-law or Pottstown, Pa. On page 2 Bryan and Roosevelt are succeeded by certain heavy stuff in the Petroleum V. Nasby manner upon the condition of obstetrics, pediatrics and the allied sciences among whales. Page 3 starts off with the old jocosity to the effect that people talk too much about the weather. It progresses or resolves, as the musicians say, into the wheeze to the effect that people like to dispute over what is the best thing to eat for breakfast. On page 4 we come to what musicians would call the formal statement of the main theme—that is, of the how-I-like-to-talk-of-my-operation motif. We have thus covered four pages.

Page 5 starts out with an enharmonic change: to wit, from the idea that ex-patients like to talk of their operations to the idea that patients in being like to swap symptoms. Following this there is a repetition of the gold theme—that is, the theme of the doctor's bill. On page 6 there are two chuckles. One springs out of a reference to "light housekeeping," a phrase which invariably strikes an American vaudeville audience as salaciously whimsical. The other is grounded upon the well-known desire of baseball fans to cut the umpire's throat. On page 6 there enters for the first time what may be called the second theme of the book. This is the whiskers motif. The whole of this page, with the exception of a sentence embodying the old wheeze about the happy times before germs were invented, is given over to variations of the whiskers joke. Page 8 continues this development section. Whiskers of various fantastic varieties are mentioned—trellis whiskers, bosky whiskers, ambush whiskers, loose, luxuriant whiskers, landscaped whiskers, whiskers that are winter quarters for pathogenic organisms. Some hard, hard squeezing, and the humor in whiskers is temporarily exhausted. Page 8 closes with the old joke about the cruel thumping which doctors perform upon their patients' clavicles.

Now for page 9. It opens with a third statement of the gold motif—"He then took my temperature and $15." Following comes the dentist's office motif —that is, the motif of reluctance, of oozing courage, of flight. At the bottom of the page the gold motif is repeated in the key of E minor. Pages 10 and 11 are devoted to simple description, with very little effort at humor. On page 12 there is a second statement, for the full brass choir, of the dentist's office motif. On page 13 there are more echoes from Petroleum V. Nasby, the subject this time being a man "who got his spleen back from the doctor's and now keeps it in a bottle of alcohol." On page 14 one finds the innocent bystander joke; on page 15 the joke about the terrifying effects of reading a patent medicine almanac. Also, at the bottom of the page, there is a third statement of the dentist's office joke. On page 16 it gives way to a restatement of the whiskers theme, in augmentation, which in turn yields to the third or fifth restatement of the gold theme.

Let us now jump a few pages. On page 19 we come to the old joke about the talkative barber; on page 22 to the joke about the book agent; on the same page to the joke about the fashionableness of appendicitis; on page 23 to the joke about the clumsy carver who projects the turkey's gizzard into the visiting pastor's eye; on page 28 to a restatement of the barber joke; on page 31 to another statement—is it the fifth or sixth?—of the dentist's office joke; on page 37 to the katzenjammer joke; on page 39 to the old joke about doctors burying their mistakes. . . . And so on. And so on and so on. And so on and so on and so on. On pages 48 and 49 there is a perfect riot of old jokes, including the *n*th variation of the whiskers joke and a fearful and wonderful pun about Belgian hares and heirs. . . .

On second thoughts I go no further. . . . This, remember, is the book that Cobb's publishers, apparently with his own *Nihil Obstat*, choose at his best. This is the official masterpiece of the "new Mark Twain." Nevertheless, even so laboriously flabby a farceur has his moments. I turn to Frank J. Wilstach's Dictionary of Similes and find this credited to him: "No more privacy than a goldfish." Here, at last, is something genuinely humorous. Here, moreover, is something apparently new.

VIII. HERMANN SUDERMANN

THE fact that Sudermann is the author of the most successful play that has come out of Germany since the collapse of the romantic movement is the most eloquent of all proofs, perhaps, of his lack of force and originality as a dramatist. "Heimat," Englished, Frenched and Italianized as "Magda," gave a new and gaudy leading rôle to all the middle-aged chewers of scenery; they fell upon it as upon a new Marguerite Gautier, and with it they coaxed the tears of all nations. That was in the middle nineties. To-day the piece seems almost as old-fashioned as "The Princess Bonnie," and even in Germany it has gone under the counter. If it is brought out at all, it is to adorn the death agonies of some doddering star of the last generation.

Sudermann was one of the first deer flushed by Arno Holz and Johannes Schlaf, the founders of German naturalism. He had written a couple of successful novels, "Frau Sorge" and "Der Katzensteg," before the *Uberbrettl'* got on its legs, and so he was a recruit worth snaring. The initial fruit of his enlistment was "Die Ehre," a *reductio ad absurdum* of

Prussian notions of honor, as incomprehensible outside of Germany as Franz Adam Beyerlein's "Zapfen-
streich" or Carl Bleibtreu's "Die Edelsten der Nation." Then followed "Sodoms Ende," and after it,
"Heimat." Already the emptiness of naturalism was
beginning to oppress Sudermann, as it was also op-
pressing Hauptmann. The latter, in 1892, re-
bounded from it to the unblushing romanticism of
"Hanneles Himmelfahrt." As for Sudermann, he
chose to temper the rigors of the Schlaf-Holz formula
(by Ibsen out of Zola) with sardoodledum. The result was this "Heimat," in which naturalism was
wedded to a mellow sentimentality, caressing to au-
diences bred upon the drama of perfumed adultery.
The whole last scene of the play, indeed, was no more
than an echo of Augier's "Le Mariage d' Olympe."
It is no wonder that even Sarah Bernhardt pronounced
it a great work.

Since then Sudermann has wobbled, and in the novel
as well as in the drama. Lacking the uncanny versa-
tility of Hauptmann, he has been unable to conquer the
two fields of romance and reality. Instead he has lost
himself between them, a rat without a tail. "Das hohe
Lied," his most successful novel since "Frau Sorge,"
is anything but a first-rate work. Its opening chapter
is a superlatively fine piece of writing, but after that
he grows uncertain of his way, and toward the end
one begins to wonder what it is all about. No coher-

ent idea is in it; it is simply a sentimentalization of the unpleasant; if it were not for the naughtiness of some of the scenes no one would read it. An American dramatist has made a play of it—a shocker for the same clowns who were entranced by Brieux's "Les Avariés."

The trouble with Sudermann, here and elsewhere, is that he has no sound underpinnings, and is a bit uncertain about his characters and his story. He starts off furiously, let us say, as a Zola, and then dilutes Zolaism with romance, and then pulls himself up and begins to imitate Ibsen, and then trips and falls headlong into the sugar bowl of sentimentality. Lily Czepanek, in "Das hohe Lied," swoons at critical moments, like the heroine of a tale for chambermaids. It is almost as if Lord Jim should get converted at a gospel mission, or Nora Helmer let down her hair. . . . But these are defects in Sudermann the novelist and dramatist, and in that Sudermann only. In the short story they conceal themselves; he is done before he begins to vacillate. In this field, indeed, all his virtues—of brisk, incisive writing, of flashing observation, of dexterous stage management, of emotional fire and address—have a chance to show themselves, and without any wearing thin. The book translated as "The Indian Lily" contains some of the best short stories that German—or any other language, for that matter—can offer. They are mordant, succinct and extraordinarily vivid character studies, each full of penetrating irony and sardonic pity, each with the chill wind of disillusion blowing through it, each preaching that life is a hideous farce, that good and bad are almost meaningless words, that truth is only the lie that is easiest to believe. . . .

It is hard to choose between stories so high in merit, but surely "The Purpose" is one of the best. Of all the latter-day Germans, only Ludwig Thoma, in "Ein bayrischer Soldat," has ever got a more brilliant reality into a crowded space. Here, in less than fifteen thousand words, Sudermann rehearses the tragedy of a whole life, and so great is the art of the thing that one gets a sense of perfect completeness, almost of exhaustiveness. . . . Antonie Wiesner, the daughter of a country innkeeper, falls in love with Robert Messerschmidt, a medical student, and they sin the scarlet sin. To Robert, perhaps, the thing is a mere interlude of midsummer, but to Toni it is all life's meaning and glory. Robert is poor and his degree is still two years ahead; it is out of the question for him to marry. Very well, Toni will find a father for her child; she is her lover's property, and that property must be protected. And she will wait willingly, careless of the years, for the distant day of triumph and redemption. All other ideas and ideals drop out of her mind; she becomes an automaton moved by the one impulse, the one yearning. She marries one

Wiegand, a decayed innkeeper; he, poor fool, accepts the parentage of her child. Her father, rich and unsuspicious, buys them a likely inn; they begin to make money. And then begins the second chapter of Toni's sacrifice. She robs her husband systematically and steadily; she takes commissions on all his goods; she becomes the houri of his bar, that trade may grow and pickings increase. Mark by mark, the money goes to Robert. It sees him through the university; it gives him his year or two in the hospitals; it buys him a practice; it feeds and clothes him, and his mother with him. The months and years pass endlessly—a young doctor's progress is slow. But finally the great day approaches. Soon Robert will be ready for his wife. But Wiegand—what of him? Toni thinks of half a dozen plans. The notion of poisoning him gradually formulates itself. Not a touch of horror stays her. She is, by this time, beyond all the common moralities—a monomaniac with no thought for anything save her great purpose. But an accident saves Wiegand. Toni, too elaborate in her plans, poisons herself by mischance, and comes near dying. Very well, if not poison, then some more subtle craft. She puts a barmaid into Wiegand's path; she manages the whole affair; before long she sees her victim safely enmeshed. A divorce follows; the inn is sold; her father's death makes her suddenly rich—at last she is off to greet her lord!

That meeting! . . . Toni waits in the little flat that she has rented in the city—she and her child, the child of Robert. Robert is to come at noon; as the slow moments pass the burden of her happiness seems too great to bear. And then suddenly the ecstatic climax—the ring at the door. . . . "A gentleman entered. A strange gentleman. Wholly strange. Had she met him on the street she would not have known him. He had grown old—forty, fifty, a hundred years. Yet his real age could not be over twenty-eight! . . . He had grown fat. He carried a little paunch around with him, round and comfortable. And the honorable scars gleamed in round, red cheeks. His eyes seemed small and receding. . . . And when he said: 'Here I am at last,' it was no longer the old voice, clear and a little resonant, which had echoed and reëchoed in her spiritual ear. He gurgled as though he had swallowed dumplings." An oaf without and an oaf within! Toni is for splendors, triumphs, the life; Robert has "settled down." His remote village, hard by the Russian border, is to his liking; he has made comfortable friends there; he is building up a practice. He is, of course, a man of honor. He will marry Toni— willingly and with gratitude, even with genuine affection. Going further, he will pay back to her every cent that ever came from Wiegand's till. He has kept a strict account. Here it is, in a little blue note-

book—seven years of entries. As he reads them
aloud the events of those seven years unroll themselves before Toni and every mark brings up its
picture—stolen cash and trinkets, savings in railroad
fares and food, commissions upon furniture and
wines, profits of champagne debauches with the county
councilor, sharp trading in milk and eggs, "suspense
and longing, an inextricable web of falsification and
trickery, of terror and lying without end. The
memory of no guilt is spared her." Robert is an
honest, an honorable man. He has kept a strict account; the money is waiting in bank. What is more,
he will make all necessary confessions. He has not,
perhaps, kept to the letter of fidelity. There was a
waitress in Berlin; there was a nurse at the surgical
clinic; there is even now a Lithuanian servant girl
at his bachelor quarters. The last named, of course,
will be sent away forthwith. Robert is a man of
honor, a man sensitive to every requirement of the
punctilio, a gentleman. He will order the announce-
ment cards, consult a clergyman—and not forget to get
rid of the Lithuanian and air the house. . . . Poor
Toni stares at him as he departs. "Will he come back
soon?" asks the child. "I scarcely think so," she
answers. . . . "That night she broke the purpose of
her life, the purpose that had become interwoven with
a thousand others, and when the morning came she
wrote a letter of farewell to the beloved of her youth."

A short story of rare and excellent quality. A short story—oh, miracle!—worth reading twice. It is not so much that its motive is new—that motive, indeed, has appeared in fiction many times, though usually with the man as the protagonist—as that its workmanship is superb. Sudermann here shows that, for all his failings elsewhere, he knows superlatively how to write. His act divisions are exactly right; his *scènes à faire* are magnificently managed; he has got into the thing that rhythmic ebb and flow of emotion which makes for great drama. And in most of the other stories in this book you will find much the same skill. No other, perhaps, is quite so good as "The Purpose," but at least one of them, "The Song of Death," is not far behind. Here we have the tragedy of a woman brought up rigorously, puritanically, stupidly, who discovers, just as it is too late, that love may be a wild dance, an ecstasy, an orgy. I can imagine no more grotesquely pathetic scene than that which shows this drab preacher's wife watching by her husband's death-bed—while through the door comes the sound of amorous delirium from the next room. And then there is a strangely moving Christmas story, "Merry Folk"—pathos with the hard iron in it. And there are "Autumn" and "The Indian Lily," elegies to lost youth—the first of them almost a fit complement to Joseph Conrad's great paean to youth triumphant.

Altogether, a collection of short stories of the very first rank. Write off "Das hohe Lied," "Frau Sorge" and all the plays: a Sudermann remains who must be put in a high and honorable place, and will be remembered.

IX. GEORGE ADE

WHEN, after the Japs and their vassals conquer us and put us to the sword, and the republic descends into hell, some literary don of Oxford or Mittel-Europa proceeds to the predestined autopsy upon our Complete Works, one of the things he will surely notice, reviewing our literary history, is the curious persistence with which the dons native to the land have overlooked its emerging men of letters. I mean, of course, its genuine men of letters, its salient and truly original men, its men of intrinsic and unmistakable distinction. The fourth-raters have fared well enough, God knows. Go back to any standard literature book of ten, or twenty, or thirty, or fifty years ago, and you will be amazed by its praise of shoddy mediocrities, long since fly-blown and forgotten. George William Curtis, now seldom heard of at all, save perhaps in the reminiscences of senile publishers, was treated in his day with all the deference due to a prince of the blood. Artemus Ward, Petroleum V. Nasby and half a dozen other such hollow buffoons were ranked with Mark Twain, and even above him. Frank R.

Stockton, for thirty years, was the delight of all right-thinking reviewers. Richard Henry Stoddard and Edmund Clarence Stedman were eminent personages, both as critics and as poets. And Donald G. Mitchell, to make an end of dull names, bulked so grandly in the academic eye that he was snatched from his tear-jugs and his tea-pots to become a charter member of the National Institute of Arts and Letters, and actually died a member of the American Academy!

Meanwhile, three of the five indubitably first-rate artists that America has produced went quite without orthodox recognition at home until either foreign enthusiasm or domestic clamor from below forced them into a belated and grudging sort of notice. I need not say that I allude to Poe, Whitman and Mark Twain. If it ever occurred to any American critic of position, during Poe's lifetime, that he was a greater man than either Cooper or Irving, then I have been unable to find any trace of the fact in the critical literature of the time. The truth is that he was looked upon as a facile and somewhat dubious journalist, too cocksure by half, and not a man to be encouraged. Lowell praised him in 1845 and at the same time denounced the current over-praise of lesser men, but later on this encomium was diluted with very important reservations, and there the matter stood until Baudelaire discovered the poet and his belated fame came winging home. Whitman, as every one

knows, fared even worse. Emerson first hailed him
and then turned tail upon him, eager to avoid any
share in his ill-repute among blockheads. No other
critic of any influence gave him help. He was carried through his dark days of poverty and persecution by a few private enthusiasts, none of them with
the ear of the public, and in the end it was Frenchmen
and Englishmen who lifted him into the light. Imagine a Harvard professor lecturing upon him in 1865!
As for Mark Twain, the story of his first fifteen years
has been admirably told by Prof. Dr. William Lyon
Phelps, of Yale. The dons were unanimously against
him. Some sneered at him as a feeble mountebank;
others refused to discuss him at all; not one harbored
the slightest suspicion that he was a man of genius,
or even one leg of a man of genius. Phelps makes
merry over this academic attempt to dispose of Mark
by putting him into Coventry—and himself joins the
sanctimonious brethren who essay the same enterprise
against Dreiser. . . .

I come by this route to George Ade—who perhaps
fails to fit into the argument doubly, for on the one
hand he is certainly not a literary artist of the first
rank, and on the other hand he has long enjoyed a
meed of appreciation and even of honor, for the National Institute of Arts and Letters elevated him to
its gilt-edged purple in its first days, and he is still on
its roll of men of "notable achievement in art, music

or literature," along with Robert W. Chambers, Henry
Sydnor Harrison, Oliver Herford, E. S. Martin and
E. W. Townsend, author of "Chimmie Fadden."
Nevertheless, he does not fall too far outside, after
all, for if he is not of the first rank then he surely deserves a respectable place in the second rank, and if
the National Institute broke the spell by admitting
him then it was probably on the theory that he was a
second Chambers or Herford, or maybe even a second Martin or Townsend.   As for the text-book dons,
they hold resolutely to the doctrine that he scarcely
exists, and is not worth noticing at all.   For example,
there is Prof. Fred Lewis Pattee, author of "A History of American Literature Since 1870."   Prof.
Pattee notices Chambers, Marion Harland, Herford,
Townsend, Amélie Rives, R. K. Munkittrick and many
other such ornaments of the national letters, and even
has polite bows for Gelett Burgess, Carolyn Wells
and John Kendrick Bangs, but the name of Ade is
missing from his index, as is that of Dreiser.   So
with the other pedagogues.   They are unanimously
shy of Ade in their horn-books for sophomores, and
they are gingery in their praise of him in their innumerable review articles.   He is commended, when
at all, much as the late Joseph Jefferson used to be
commended—that is, to the accompaniment of reminders that even a clown is one of God's creatures,
and may have the heart of a Christian under his

motley. The most laudatory thing ever said of him by any critic of the apostolic succession, so far as I can discover, is that he is clean—that he does not import the lewd buffooneries of the barroom, the smoking-car and the wedding reception into his books. . . .

But what are the facts? The facts are that Ade is one of the few genuinely original literary craftsmen now in practice among us; that he comes nearer to making literature, when he has full steam up, than any save a scant half-dozen of our current novelists, and that the whole body of his work, both in books and for the stage, is as thoroughly American, in cut and color, in tang and savor, in structure and point of view, as the work of Howells, E. W. Howe or Mark Twain. No single American novel that I can think of shows half the sense of nationality, the keen feeling for national prejudice and peculiarity, the sharp and pervasive Americanism of such Adean fables as "The Good Fairy of the Eighth Ward and the Dollar Excursion of the Steam-Fitters," "The Mandolin Players and the Willing Performer," and "The Adult Girl Who Got Busy Before They Could Ring the Bell on Her." Here, amid a humor so grotesque that it almost tortures the midriff, there is a startlingly vivid and accurate evocation of the American scene. Here, under all the labored extravagance, there are brilliant flashlight pictures of the American people, and Ameri-

can ways of thinking, and the whole of American
Kultur. Here the veritable Americano stands forth,
lacking not a waggery, a superstition, a snuffle or a
wen.

Ade himself, for all his story-teller's pretense of
remoteness, is as absolutely American as any of his
prairie-town traders and pushers, Shylocks and Dog-
berries, beaux and belles. No other writer of our
generation, save perhaps Howe, is more unescapably
national in his every gesture and trick of mind. He
is as American as buckwheat cakes, or the Knights of
Pythias, or the chautauqua, or Billy Sunday, or a
bull by Dr. Wilson. He fairly reeks of the national
Philistinism, the national respect for respectability,
the national distrust of ideas. He is a marcher, one
fancies, in parades; he joins movements, and movements against movements; he knows no language save
his own; he regards a Roosevelt quite seriously and a
Mozart or an Ibsen as a joke; one would not be surprised to hear that, until he went off to his fresh-water
college, he slept in his underwear and read the *Epworth Herald.* But, like Dreiser, he is a peasant
touched by the divine fire; somehow, a great instinctive artist got himself born out there on that lush
Indiana farm. He has the rare faculty of seeing accurately, even when the thing seen is directly under
his nose, and he has the still rarer faculty of recording
vividly, of making the thing seen move with life.

One often doubts a character in a novel, even in a good novel, but who ever doubted Gus in "The Two Mandolin Players," or Mae in "Sister Mae," or, to pass from the fables, Payson in "Mr. Payson's Satirical Christmas"? Here, with strokes so crude and obvious that they seem to be laid on with a broom, Ade achieves what O. Henry, with all his ingenuity, always failed to achieve: he fills his bizarre tales with human beings. There is never any artfulness on the surface. The tale itself is never novel, or complex; it never surprises; often it is downright banal. But underneath there is an artfulness infinitely well wrought, and that is the artfulness of a story-teller who dredges his story out of his people, swiftly and skillfully, and does not squeeze his people into his story, laboriously and unconvincingly.

Needless to say, a moralist stands behind the comedian. He would teach; he even grows indignant. Roaring like a yokel at a burlesque show over such wild and light-hearted jocosities as "Paducah's Favorite Comedians" and "Why 'Gondola' Was Put Away," one turns with something of a start to such things as "Little Lutie," "The Honest Money Maker" and "The Corporation Director and the Mislaid Ambition." Up to a certain point it is all laughter, but after that there is a flash of the knife, a show of teeth. Here a national limitation often closes in upon the satirist. He cannot quite separate the unaccustomed from the

abominable; he is unable to avoid rattling his Philis-
tine trappings a bit proudly; he must prove that he,
too, is a right-thinking American, a solid citizen and
a patriot, unshaken in his lofty rectitude by such
poisons as aristocracy, adultery, *hors d'œuvres* and
the sonata form. But in other directions this thor-
ough-going nationalism helps him rather than hinders
him. It enables him, for one thing, to see into sentimentality, and to comprehend it and project it accurately. I know of no book which displays the mooni-
ness of youth with more feeling and sympathy than
"Artie," save it be Frank Norris' forgotten "Blix."
In such fields Ade achieves a success that is rare and
indubitable. He makes the thing charming and he
makes it plain.

But all these fables and other compositions of his
are mere sketches, inconsiderable trifles, impromptus
in bad English, easy to write and of no importance!
Are they, indeed? Do not believe it for a moment.
Fifteen or twenty years ago, when Ade was at the
height of his celebrity as a newspaper Sganarelle,
scores of hack comedians tried to imitate him—and
all failed. I myself was of the number. I operated
a so-called funny column in a daily newspaper, and
like my colleagues near and far, I essayed to manufac-
ture fables in slang. What miserable botches they
were! How easy it was to imitate Ade's manner—
and how impossible to imitate his matter! No; please

don't get the notion that it is a simple thing to write
such a fable as that of "The All-Night Seance and the
Limit That Ceased to Be," or that of "The Preacher
Who Flew His Kite, But Not Because He Wished to Do
So," or that of "The Roystering Blades." Far from
it! On the contrary, the only way you will ever
accomplish the feat will be by first getting Ade's firm
grasp upon American character, and his ability to
think out a straightforward, simple, amusing story,
and his alert feeling for contrast and climax, and his
extraordinary talent for devising novel, vivid and unforgettable phrases. Those phrases of his sometimes
wear the external vestments of a passing slang, but
they are no more commonplace and vulgar at bottom
than Gray's "mute, inglorious Milton" or the "some-
wheres East of Suez" of Kipling. They reduce an
idea to a few pregnant syllables. They give the attention a fillip and light up a whole scene in a flash.
They are the running evidences of an eye that sees
clearly and of a mind that thinks shrewdly. They
give distinction to the work of a man who has so well
concealed a highly complex and efficient artistry that
few have ever noticed it.

X. THE BUTTE BASHKIRTSEFF

OF all the pseudo-rebels who have raised a tarletan black flag in These States, surely Mary MacLane is one of the most pathetic. When, at nineteen, she fluttered Vassar with "The Story of Mary MacLane," the truth about her was still left somewhat obscure; the charm of her flapperhood, so to speak, distracted attention from it, and so concealed it. But when, at thirty-five, she achieved "I, Mary MacLane," it emerged crystal-clear; she had learned to describe her malady accurately, though she still wondered, a bit wistfully, just what it was. And that malady? That truth? Simply that a Scotch Presbyterian with a soaring soul is as cruelly beset as a wolf with fleas, a zebra with the botts. Let a spark of the divine fire spring to life in that arid corpse, and it must fight its way to flame through a drum fire of wet sponges. A humming bird immersed in *Kartoffelsuppe*. Walter Pater writing for the London *Daily Mail*. Lucullus traveling steerage. . . . A Puritan wooed and tortured by the leers of beauty, Mary MacLane in a moral republic, in a Presbyterian diocese, in Butte. . . .

I hope my figures of speech are not too abstruse. What I mean to say is simply this: that the secret of Mary MacLane is simply this: that the origin of all her inchoate naughtiness is simply this: that she is a Puritan who has heard the call of joy and is struggling against it damnably. Remember so much, and the whole of her wistful heresy becomes intelligible. On the one hand the loveliness of the world enchants her; on the other hand the fires of hell warn her. This tortuous conflict accounts for her whole bag of tricks; her timorous flirtations with the devil, her occasional outbreaks of finishing-school rebellion, her hurried protestations of virginity, above all her incurable Philistinism. One need not be told that she admires the late Major General Roosevelt and Mrs. Atherton, that she wallows in the poetry of Keats. One knows quite as well that her phonograph plays the "Peer Gynt" suite, and that she is charmed by the syllogisms of G. K. Chesterton. She is, in brief, an absolutely typical American of the transition stage between Christian Endeavor and civilization. There is in her a definite poison of ideas, an æsthetic impulse that will not down—but every time she yields to it she is halted and plucked back by qualms and doubts, by the dominant superstitions of her race and time, by the dead hand of her kirk-crazy Scotch forebears.

It is precisely this grisly touch upon her shoulder

that stimulates her to those naïve explosions of scandalous confidence which make her what she is. If there were no sepulchral voice in her ear, warning her that it is the mark of a hussy to be kissed by a man with "iron-gray hair, a brow like Apollo and a jowl like Bill Sykes," she would not confess it and boast of it, as she does on page 121 of "I, Mary MacLane." If it were not a Presbyterian axiom that a lady who says "damn" is fit only to join the white slaves, she would not pen a defiant Damniad, as she does on pages 108, 109 and 110. And if it were not held universally in Butte that sex passion is the exclusive infirmity of the male, she would not blab out in meeting that—but here I get into forbidden waters and had better refer you to page 209. It is not the godless voluptuary who patronizes leg-shows and the cabaret; it is the Methodist deacon with unaccustomed vine-leaves in his hair. It is not genuine artists, serving beauty reverently and proudly, who herd in Greenwich Village and bawl for art; it is precisely a mob of Middle Western Baptists to whom the very idea of art is still novel, and intoxicating, and more than a little bawdy. And to make an end, it is not cocottes who read the highly-spiced magazines which burden all the book-stalls; it is sedentary married women who, while faithful to their depressing husbands in the flesh, yet allow their imaginations to play furtively upon the charms of theoretical intrigues with such pretty fellows as Francis X. Bushman, Enrico Caruso and Vincent Astor.

An understanding of this plain fact not only explains the MacLane and her gingery carnalities of the chair; it also explains a good part of latter-day American literature. That literature is the self-expression of a people who have got only half way up the ladder leading from moral slavery to intellectual freedom. At every step there is a warning tug, a protest from below. Sometimes the climber docilely drops back; sometimes he emits a petulant defiance and reaches boldly for the next round. It is this occasional defiance which accounts for the periodical efflorescence of mere school-boy naughtiness in the midst of our oleaginous virtue—for the shouldering out of the *Ladies' Home Journal* by magazines of adultery all compact—for the provocative baring of calf and scapula by women who regard it as immoral to take Benedictine with their coffee—for the peopling of Greenwich Village by oafs who think it a devilish adventure to victual in cellars, and read Krafft-Ebing, and stare at the corset-scarred nakedness of decadent cloak-models.

I have said that the climber is but half way up the ladder. I wish I could add that he is moving ahead, but the truth is that he is probably quite stationary. We have our spasms of revolt, our flarings up of peek-

aboo waists, free love and "art," but a mighty back-
wash of piety fetches each and every one of them soon
or late. A mongrel and inferior people, incapable of
any spiritual aspiration above that of second-rate English colonials, we seek refuge inevitably in the one
sort of superiority that the lower castes of men can
authentically boast, to wit, superiority in docility, in
credulity, in resignation, in morals. We are the most
moral race in the world; there is not another that we
do not look down upon in that department; our con-
fessed aim and destiny as a nation is to inoculate them
all with our incomparable rectitude. In the last
analysis, all ideas are judged among us by moral
standards; moral values are our only permanent tests
of worth, whether in the arts, in politics, in philosophy
or in life itself. Even the instincts of man, so intrinsically immoral, so innocent, are fitted with moral
false-faces. That bedevilment by sex ideas which
punishes continence, so abhorrent to nature, is converted into a moral frenzy, pathological in the end.
The impulse to cavort and kick up one's legs, so
healthy, so universal, is hedged in by incomprehensible taboos; it becomes stealthy, dirty, degrading.
The desire to create and linger over beauty, the sign
and touchstone of man's rise above the brute, is held
down by doubts and hesitations; when it breaks
through it must do so by orgy and explosion, half lu-

dicrous and half pathetic.   Our function, we choose to believe, is to teach and inspire the world.   We are wrong.   Our function is to amuse the world.   We are the Bryan, the Henry Ford, the Billy Sunday among the nations. . . .

XI. SIX MEMBERS OF THE INSTITUTE

1

The Boudoir Balzac

THE late Percival Pollard was, in my nonage, one of my enthusiasms, and, later on, one of my friends. How, as a youngster, I used to lie in wait for the *Criterion* every week, and devour Pollard, Huneker, Meltzer and Vance Thompson! That was in the glorious middle nineties and savory pots were brewing. Scarcely a week went by without a new magazine of some unearthly *Tendenz* or other appearing on the stands; scarcely a month failed to bring forth its new genius. Pollard was up to his hips in the movement. He had a hand for every débutante. He knew everything that was going on. Polyglot, catholic, generous, alert, persuasive, forever oscillating between New York and Paris, London and Berlin, he probably covered a greater territory in the one art of letters than Huneker covered in all seven. He worked so hard as introducer of intellectual ambassadors, in fact, that he never had time to write his own books. One very brilliant volume,

"Masks and Minstrels of New Germany," adequately represents him. The rest of his criticism, clumsily dragged from the files of the *Criterion* and *Town Topics*, is thrown together ineptly in "Their Day in Court." Death sneaked upon him from behind; he was gone before he could get his affairs in order. I shall never forget his funeral—no doubt a fit finish for a critic. Not one of the authors he had whooped and battled for was present—not one, that is, save old Ambrose Bierce. Bierce came in an elegant plug-hat and told me some curious anecdotes on the way to the crematory, chiefly of morgues, dissecting-rooms and lonely church-yards: he was the most gruesome of men. A week later, on a dark, sleety Christmas morning, I returned to the crematory, got the ashes, and shipped them West. Pollard awaits the Second Coming of his Redeemer in Iowa, hard by the birthplace of Prof. Dr. Stuart P. Sherman. Well, let us not repine. Huneker lives in Flatbush and was born in Philadelphia. Cabell is a citizen of Richmond, Va. Willa Sibert Cather was once one of the editors of *McClure's Magazine*. Dreiser, before his annunciation, edited dime novels for Street & Smith, and will be attended by a Methodist friar, I daresay, on the gallows. . . .

Pollard, as I say, was a man I respected. He knew a great deal. Half English, half German and wholly cosmopolitan, he brought valuable knowledges and enthusiasms to the developing American literature of his time. Moreover, I had affection for him as well as respect, for he was a capital companion at the *Biertisch* and was never too busy to waste a lecture on my lone ear—say on Otto Julius Bierbaum (one of his friends), or Anatole France, or the technic of the novel, or the scoundrelism of publishers. It thus pains me to violate his tomb—but let his shade forgive me as it hopes to be forgiven! For it was Pollard, I believe, who set going the doctrine that Robert W. Chambers is a man of talent—a bit too commercial, perhaps, but still fundamentally a man of talent. You will find it argued at length in "Their Day in Court." There Pollard called the roll of the "promising young men" of the time, *circa* 1908. They were Winston Churchill, David Graham Phillips—and Chambers! Alas, for all prophets and their prognostications! Phillips, with occasional reversions to honest work, devoted most of his later days to sensational serials for the train-boy magazines, and when he died his desk turned out to be full of them, and they kept dribbling along for three or four years. Churchill, seduced by the uplift, has become an evangelist and a bore—a worse case, even, than that of H. G. Wells. And Chambers? Let the New York *Times* answer. Here, in all sobriety, is its description of the heroine of "The Moonlit Way," one of his latest pieces:

She is a lovely and fascinating dancer who, before the war, held the attention of all Europe and incited a great many men who had nothing better to do to fall in love with her. She bursts upon the astonished gaze of several of the important characters of the story when she dashes into the ballroom of the German Embassy *standing upon a bridled ostrich,* which she compels to dance and go through its paces at her command. She is dressed, Mr. Chambers assures us, *in nothing but the skin of her virtuous youth, modified slightly by a yashmak and a zone of blue jewels about her hips and waist.*

The italics are mine. I wonder what poor Pollard would think of it. He saw the shoddiness in Chambers, the leaning toward "profitable pot-boiling," but he saw, too, a fundamental earnestness and a high degree of skill. What has become of these things? Are they visible, even as ghosts, in the preposterous serials that engaud the magazines of Mr. Hearst, and then load the department-stores as books? Were they, in fact, ever there at all? Did Pollard observe them, or did he merely imagine them? I am inclined to think that he merely imagined them—that his delight in what he described as "many admirable tricks" led him into a fatuity that he now has an eternity to regret. Chambers grows sillier and sillier, emptier and emptier, worse and worse. But was he ever more than a fifth-rater? I doubt it. Let us go back half a dozen years, to the days before the war forced the pot-boiler down into utter imbecility. I choose, at random, "The Gay Rebellion." Here is a specimen of the dialogue:

"It startled me. How did I know what it might have been? It might have been a bear—or a cow."

"You talk," said Sayre angrily, "like William Dean Howells! Haven't you *any* romance in you?"

"Not what *you* call romance. Pass the flapjacks." Sayre passed them.

"My attention," he said, "instantly became riveted upon the bushes. I strove to pierce them with a piercing glance. Suddenly—"

"Sure! 'Suddenly' always comes next."

"Suddenly . . . the leaves were stealthily parted, and—"

"A naked savage in full war paint—"

"Naked nothing! a young girl in—a perfectly fitting gown stepped noiselessly out."

"Out of what, you gink?"

"The bushes, dammit! . . . She looked at me; I gazed at her. Somehow—"

"In plainer terms, she gave you the eye. What?"

"That's a peculiarly coarse observation."

"Then tell it in your own way."

"I will. The sunlight fell softly upon the trees of the ancient wood."

"*Woodn't* that bark you!"

And so on, and so on, for page after page. Can you imagine more idiotic stuff—"pierce and piercing," "you gink," "she gave you the eye," "*woodn't* that bark you?" One is reminded of horrible things

—the repartees of gas-house comedians in vaudeville, the whimsical editorials in *Life,* the forbidding ghouleries of Irvin Cobb among jokes pale and clammy in death. . . . But let us, you may say, go back a bit further—back to the days of the *Chap-Book.* There was then, perhaps, a far different Chambers—a fellow of sound talent and artistic self-respect, well deserving the confidence and encouragement of Pollard. Was there, indeed? If you think so, go read "The King in Yellow," *circa* 1895—if you can. I myself, full of hope, have tried it. In it I have found drivel almost as dull as that, say, in "Ailsa Page."

2

A Stranger on Parnassus

The case of Hamlin Garland belongs to pathos in the grand manner, as you will discover on reading his autobiography, "A Son of the Middle Border." What ails him is a vision of beauty, a seductive strain of bawdy music over the hills. He is a sort of male Mary MacLane, but without either Mary's capacity for picturesque blasphemy or her skill at plain English. The vision, in his youth, tore him from his prairie plow and set him to clawing the anthills at the foot of Parnassus. He became an elocutionist—what, in modern times, would be called a chautauquan. He aspired to write for the *Atlantic Monthly.* He fell under the spell of the Boston *aluminados* of 1885, which is as if one were to take fire from a June-bug. Finally, after embracing the Single Tax, he achieved a couple of depressing story-books, earnest, honest and full of indignation.

American criticism, which always mistakes a poignant document for æsthetic form and organization, greeted these moral volumes as works of art, and so Garland found himself an accepted artist and has made shift to be an artist ever since. No more grotesque miscasting of a diligent and worthy man is recorded in profane history. He has no more feeling for the intrinsic dignity of beauty, no more comprehension of it as a thing in itself, than a policeman. He is, and always has been, a moralist endeavoring ineptly to translate his messianic passion into æsthetic terms, and always failing. "A Son of the Middle Border," undoubtedly the best of all his books, projects his failure brilliantly. It is, in substance, a document of considerable value—a naïve and often highly illuminating contribution to the history of the American peasantry. It is, in form, a thoroughly third-rate piece of writing—amateurish, flat, banal, repellent. Garland gets facts into it; he gets the relentless sincerity of the rustic Puritan; he gets a sort of evangelical passion. But he doesn't get any charm. He doesn't get any beauty.

In such a career, as in such a book, there is some-

thing profoundly pathetic.   One follows the progress
of the man with a constant sense that he is steering
by faulty compasses, that fate is leading him into
paths too steep and rocky—nay, too dark and lovely—
for him.   An awareness of beauty is there, and a
wistful desire to embrace it, but the confident gusto
of the artist is always lacking.   What one encounters
in its place is the enthusiasm of the pedagogue, the
desire to yank the world up to the soaring Methodist
level, the hot yearning to displace old ideas with new
ideas, and usually much worse ideas, for example, the
Single Tax and spook-chasing.   The natural goal of
the man was the evangelical stump.   He was led
astray when those Boston Brahmins of the last generation, enchanted by his sophomoric platitudes about
Shakespeare, set him up as a critic of the arts, and
then as an imaginative artist.   He should have gone
back to the saleratus belt, taken to the chautauquas,
preached his foreordained perunas, got himself into
Congress, and so helped to save the republic from the
demons that beset it.   What a gladiator he would
have made against the Plunderbund, the White Slave
Traffic, the Rum Demon, the Kaiser!   What a rival
to the Hon. Claude Kitchin, the Rev. Dr. Newell
Dwight Hillis!

His worst work, I daresay, is in some of his fiction—for example, in "The Forester's Daughter."
But my own favorite among his books is "The Shadow

World," a record of his communings with the gaseous precipitates of the departed. He takes great pains at the start to assure us that he is a man of alert intelligence and without prejudices or superstitions. He has no patience, it appears, with those idiots who swallow the buffooneries of spiritualist mediums too greedily. For him the scientific method—the method which examines all evidence cynically and keeps on doubting until the accumulated proof, piled mountain-high, sweeps down in an overwhelming avalanche. . . . Thus he proceeds to the haunted chamber and begins his dalliance with the banshees. They touch him with clammy, spectral hands; they wring music for him out of locked pianos; they throw heavy tables about the room; they give him messages from the golden shore and make him the butt of their coarse, transcendental humor. Through it all he sits tightly and solemnly, his mind open and his verdict up his sleeve. He is belligerently agnostic, and calls attention to it proudly. . . . Then, in the end, he gives himself away. One of his fellow "scientists," more frankly credulous, expresses the belief that real scientists will soon prove the existence of spooks. "I hope they will," says the agnostic Mr. Garland. . . .

Well, let us not laugh. The believing mind is a curious thing. It must absorb its endless rations of balderdash, or perish. . . . "A Son of the Middle Border" is less amusing, but a good deal more re-

spectable. It is an honest book. There is some
bragging in it, of course, but not too much. It tells an
interesting story. It radiates hard effort and earnest
purpose. . . . But what a devastating exposure of a
member of the American Academy of Arts and Letters!

3

A Merchant of Mush

Henry Sydnor Harrison is thoroughly American to
this extent: that his work is a bad imitation of something English. Find me a second-rate American in
any of the arts and I'll find you his master and pro-
totype among third, fourth or fifth-rate Englishmen.
In the present case the model is obviously W. J. Locke.
But between master and disciple there is a great gap.
Locke, at his high points, is a man of very palpable
merit. He has humor. He has ingenuity. He has
a keen eye for the pathos that so often lies in the absurd. I can discover no sign of any of these things
in Harrison's 100,000 word Christmas cards. They
are simply sentimental bosh—huge gum-drops for fat
women to snuffle over. Locke's grotesque and often
extremely amusing characters are missing; in place
of them there are the heroic cripples, silent lovers,
maudlin war veterans and angelic grandams of the
old-time Sunday-school books. The people of "V.
V.'s Eyes" are preposterous and the thesis is too silly

to be stated in plain words. No sane person would believe it if it were put into an affidavit. "Queed" is simply Locke diluted with vast drafts from "Laddie" and "Pollyanna." Queed, himself, long before the end, becomes a marionette without a toe on the ground; his Charlotte is incredible from the start. "Angela's Business" touches the bottom of the tear-jug; it would be impossible to imagine a more vapid story. Harrison, in fact, grows more mawkish book by book. He is touched, I should say, by the delusion that he has a mission to make life sweeter, to preach the Finer Things, to radiate Gladness. What! More Gladness? Another volt or two, and all civilized adults will join the Italians and Jugo-Slavs in their headlong hegira. A few more amperes, and the land will be abandoned to the Jews, the ex-Confederates and the Bolsheviki.

4

The Last of the Victorians

If William Allen White lives as long as Tennyson, and does not reform, our grandchildren will see the Victorian era gasping out its last breath in 1951. And eighty-three is no great age in Kansas, where sin is unknown. It may be, in fact, 1960, or even 1970, before the world hears the last of Honest Poverty, Chaste Affection and Manly Tears. For so long as White holds a pen these ancient sweets will be on sale at the department-store book-counters, and they will grow sweeter and sweeter, I daresay, as he works them over and over.   In his very first book of fiction there was a flavor of chewing-gum and marshmallows. In "A Certain Rich Man" the intelligent palate detected saccharine.   In "In the Heart of a Fool," his latest, the thing is carried a step further.   If you are a forward-looker and a right-thinker, if you believe that God is in His heaven and all is for the best, if you yearn to uplift and like to sob, then the volume will probably affect you, in the incomparable phrase of Clayton Hamilton, like "the music of a million Easter-lilies leaping from the grave and laughing with a silver singing."   But if you are a carnal fellow, as I am, with a stomach ruined by alcohol, it will gag you.

When I say that White is a Victorian I do not allude, of course, to the Victorianism of Thackeray and Tennyson, but to that of Felicia Hemens, of Samuel Smiles and of Dickens at his most maudlin.   Perhaps an even closer relative is to be found in "The Duchess."   White, like "The Duchess" is absolutely humorless, and, when he begins laying on the mayonnaise, absolutely shameless.   I daresay the same sort of reader admires both: the high-school girl first seized by amorous tremors, the obese multipara in her greasy kimono, the remote and weepful farm-wife.

But here a doubt intrudes itself: is it possible to imagine a woman sentimental enough to survive "In the Heart of a Fool"? I am constrained to question it. In women, once they get beyond adolescence, there is always a saving touch of irony; the life they lead infallibly makes cynics of them, though sometimes they don't know it. Observe the books they write—chiefly sardonic stuff, with heroes who are fools. Even their "glad" books, enormously successful among other women, stop far short of the sentimentality put between covers by men—for example, the aforesaid Harrison, Harold Bell Wright and the present White. Nay, it is the male sex that snuffles most and is easiest touched, particularly in America. The American man is forever falling a victim to his tender feelings. It was by that route that the collectors for the Y. M. C. A. reached him; it is thus that he is bagged incessantly by political tear-squeezers; it is precisely his softness that makes him the slave of his women-folk. What White gives him is exactly the sort of mush that is on tap in the chautauquas. "In the Heart of a Fool," like "A Certain Rich Man" is aimed deliberately and with the utmost accuracy at the delicate gizzard of the small-town yokel, the small-town yokel *male*, the horrible end-product of fifty years of Christian Endeavor, the little red schoolhouse and the direct primary.

The White formula is simple to the verge of aus-

terity.   It is, in essence, no more than a dramatization
of all the current political and sociological rumble-
bumble, by Roosevelt out of Coxey's Army, with music by the choir of the First Methodist Church.   On
the one side are the Hell Hounds of Plutocracy, the
Money Demons, the Plunderbund, and their attendant Bosses, Strike Breakers, Seducers, Nietz-
scheans, Free Lovers, Atheists and Corrupt Journalists.   On the other side are the great masses of the
plain people, and their attendant Uplifters, Good
Samaritans, Honest Workingmen, Faithful Husbands,
Inspired Dreamers and tin-horn Messiahs.   These
two armies join battle, the Bad against the Good, and
for five hundred pages or more the Good get all the
worst of it.   Their jobs are taken away from them,
their votes are bartered, their mortgages are fore-
closed, their women are debauched, their savings are
looted, their poor orphans are turned out to starve.
A sad business, surely.   One wallows in almost un-
endurable emotions.   The tears gush.   It is as affect-
ing as a movie.   Even the prose rises to a sort of
gospel-tent chant, like that of a Baptist Savonarola,
with every second sentence beginning with *and, but*
or *for.* . . . But we are already near the end, and no
escape is in sight.   Can it be that White is stumped,
like Mark Twain in his mediæval romance—that Virtue will succumb to the Interests?   Do not fear!   In
the third from the last chapter Hen Jackson, the stage-

hand, returns from the Dutchman's at the corner and throws on a rose spot-light, and then an amber, and then a violet, and then a blue. One by one the rays of Hope begin to shoot across the stage, Dr. Hamilton's Easter-lilies leap from their tomb, the *dramatis personœ* (all save the local J. Pierpont Morgan!) begin "laughing with a silver singing," and as the curtain falls the whole scene is bathed in luminiferous ether, and the professor breaks into "Onward, Christian Soldiers!" on the cabinet-organ, and there is a happy, comfortable sobbing, and an upward rolling of eyes, and a vast blowing of noses. In brief, the finish of a chautauqua lecture on "The Grand Future of America, or, The Glory of Service." In brief, slobber. . . .

It would be difficult to imagine more saccharine writing or a more mawkish and preposterous point of view. Life, as White sees it, is a purely moral phenomenon, like living pictures by the Epworth League. The virtuous are the downtrodden; the up and doing are all scoundrels. It pays to be poor and pious. Ambition is a serpent. One honest Knight of Pythias is worth ten thousand Rockefellers. The pastor is always right. So is the *Ladies' Home Journal*. The impulse that leads a young yokel of, say, twenty-two to seek marriage with a poor working-girl of, say, eighteen, is the most elevating, noble, honorable and godlike impulse native to the human consciousness. . . . Not the slightest sign of an apprehension of life as the gaudiest and most gorgeous of spectacles—not a trace of healthy delight in the eternal struggle for existence—not the faintest suggestion of Dreiser's great gusto or of Conrad's penetrating irony! Not even in the massive fact of death itself—and, like all the other Victorians, this one from the Kansas steppes is given to wholesale massacres—does he see anything mysterious, staggering, awful, inexplicable, but only an excuse for a sentimental orgy.

Alas, what would you? It is ghastly drivel, to be sure, but isn't it, after all, thoroughly American? I have an uneasy suspicion that it is—that "In the Heart of a Fool" is, at bottom, a vastly more American book than anything that James Branch Cabell has done, or Vincent O'Sullivan, or Edith Wharton, or even Howells. It springs from the heart of the land. It is the æsthetic echo of thousands of movements, of hundreds of thousands of sentimental crusades, of millions of ecstatic gospel-meetings. This is what the authentic American public, unpolluted by intelligence, wants. And this is one of the reasons why the English sniff whenever they look our way. . . .

But has White no merit? He has. He is an honest and a respectable man. He is a patriot. He trusts God. He venerates what is left of the Constitution. He once wrote a capital editorial, "What's the Matter With Kansas?" He has the knack, when

his tears are turned off, of writing a clear and grace-
ful English. . . .

5

A Bad Novelist

As I have said, it is not the artistic merit and dignity of a novel, but often simply its content as document, that makes for its success in the United States.
The criterion of truth applied to it is not the criterion
of an artist, but that of a newspaper editorial writer;
the question is not, Is it in accord with the profound-
est impulses and motives of humanity? but Is it in
accord with the current pishposh?   This accounts for
the huge popularity of such confections as Upton
Sinclair's "The Jungle" and Blasco Ibáñez's "The
Four Horsemen of the Apocalypse."   Neither had
much value as a work of art—at all events, neither
was perceptibly superior to many contemporary
novels that made no stir at all—but each had the advantage of reënforcing an emotion already aroused,
of falling into step with the procession of the moment.
Had there been no fever of muck-raking and trust
busting in 1906, "The Jungle" would have died the
death in the columns of the *Appeal to Reason,* un-
heard of by the populace in general.   And had the
United States been engaged against France instead of
for France in 1918, there would have been no argument in the literary weeklies that Blasco was a novel-

ist of the first rank and his story a masterpiece comparable to "Germinal."

Sinclair was made by "The Jungle" and has been trying his hardest to unmake himself ever since. Another of the same sort is Ernest Poole, author of "The Harbor." "The Harbor," judged by any intelligible æsthetic standard, was a bad novel. Its transactions were forced and unconvincing; its central character was shadowy and often incomprehensible; the manner of its writing was quite without distinction. But it happened to be printed at a time when the chief ideas in it had a great deal of popularity—when its vague grappling with insoluble sociological problems was the sport of all the weeklies and of half the more sober newspapers—when a nebulous, highfalutin Bolshevism was in the air—and so it excited interest and took on an aspect of profundity. That its discussion of those problems was superficial, that it said nothing new and got nowhere—all this was not an influence against its success, but an influence in favor of its success, for the sort of mind that fed upon the nebulous, professor-made politics and sociology of 1915 was the sort of mind that is chronically avid of half-truths and as chronically suspicious of forthright thinking. This has been demonstrated since that time by its easy *volte face* in the presence of emotion. The very ideas that Poole's vapid hero toyed with in 1915, to the delight of the novel-reading *intelligentsia*, would have damned the book as a pamphlet for the I. W. W., or even, perhaps, as German propaganda, three years later. But meanwhile, it had been forgotten, as novels are always forgotten, and all that remained of it was a general impression that Poole, in some way or other, was a superior fellow and to be treated with respect.

His subsequent books have tried that theory severely. "The Family" was grounded upon one of the elemental tragedies which serve a novelist most safely—the dismay of an aging man as his children drift away from him. Here was a subject full of poignant drama, and what is more, drama simple enough to develop itself without making any great demand upon the invention. Poole burdened it with too much background, and then killed it altogether by making his characters wooden. It began with a high air; it creaked and wobbled at the close; the catastrophe was quite without effect. "His Second Wife" dropped several stories lower. It turned out, on inspection, to be no more than a moral tale, feeble, wishy-washy and irritating. Everything in it—about the corrupting effects of money-lust and display, about the swinishness of cabaret "society" in New York, about the American male's absurd slavery to his women—had been said before by such gifted

Balzacs as Robert W. Chambers and Owen Johnson, and, what is more, far better said. The writing, in fact, exactly matched the theme. It was labored, artificial, dull. In the whole volume there was not a single original phrase. Once it was put down, not a scene remained in the memory, or a character. It was a cheap, a hollow and, in places, almost an idiotic book. . . .

At the time I write, this is the whole product of Poole as novelist: three novels, bad, worse, worst.

6

A Broadway Brandes

I have hitherto, in discussing White de Kansas, presented a fragile dahlia from the rhetorical garden of Clayton Hamilton, M.A. (Columbia). I now print the whole passage:

Whenever in a world-historic war the side of righteousness has triumphed, a great overflowing of art has followed soon upon the fact of victory. The noblest instincts of mankind—aroused in perilous moments fraught with intimations of mortality—have surged and soared, beneath the sunshine of a subsequent and dear-bought peace, into an immeasurable empyrean of heroic eloquence. Whenever right has circumvented might, Art has sprung alive into the world, with the music of a million Easter-lilies leaping from the grave and laughing with a silver singing.

With the highest respect for a *Magister Artium,* a pedagogue of Columbia University, a lecturer in Miss Spence's School and the Classical School for Girls, and a vice-president of the National Institute of Arts and Letters—Booh!

XII. THE GENEALOGY OF
ETIQUETTE

BARRING sociology (which is yet, of course, scarcely a science at all, but rather a monkey-shine which happens to pay, like play-acting or theology), psychology is the youngest of the sciences, and hence chiefly guesswork, empiricism, hocus-pocus, poppycock. On the one hand, there are still enormous gaps in its data, so that the determination of its simplest principles remains difficult, not to say impossible; and, on the other hand, the very hollowness and nebulosity of it, particularly around its edges, encourages a horde of quacks to invade it, sophisticate it and make nonsense of it. Worse, this state of affairs tends to such confusion of effort and direction that the quack and the honest inquirer are often found in the same man. It is, indeed, a commonplace to encounter a professor who spends his days in the laborious accumulation of psychological statistics, sticking pins into babies and platting upon a chart the ebb and flow of their yells, and his nights chasing poltergeists and other such celestial fauna over the hurdles of a spiritualist's atelier, or gazing into a crystal in the privacy of his own chamber. The Binét test and the buncombe of mesmerism are alike the children of what we roughly denominate psychology, and perhaps of equal legitimacy. Even so ingenious and competent an investigator as Prof. Dr. Sigmund Freud, who has told us a lot that is of the first importance about the materials and machinery of thought, has also told us a lot that is trivial and dubious. The essential doctrines of Freudism, no doubt, come close to the truth, but many of Freud's remoter deductions are far more scandalous than sound, and many of the professed Freudians, both American and European, have grease-paint on their noses and bladders in their hands and are otherwise quite indistinguishable from evangelists and circus clowns.

In this condition of the science it is no wonder that we find it wasting its chief force upon problems that are petty and idle when they are not downright and palpably insoluble, and passing over problems that are of immediate concern to all of us, and that might be quite readily solved, or, at any rate, considerably illuminated, by an intelligent study of the data already available. After all, not many of us care a hoot whether Sir Oliver Lodge and the Indian chief Wok-a-wok-a-mok are happy in heaven, for not many of us have any hope or desire to meet them there. Nor are we greatly excited by the discovery that, of twenty-five freshmen who are hit with clubs, 17¾ will say "Ouch!" and 22⅕ will say "Damn!"; nor by a table showing that 38.2 per centum of all men accused of homicide confess when locked up with the carcasses of their victims, including 23.4 per centum who are innocent; nor by plans and specifications, by Cagliostro out of Lucrezia Borgia, for teaching poor, God-forsaken school children to write before they can read and to multiply before they can add; nor by endless disputes between half-witted pundits as to the precise difference between perception and cognition; nor by even longer feuds, between pundits even crazier, over free will, the subconscious, the endoneurium, the functions of the corpora quadrigemina, and the meaning of dreams in which one is pursued by hyenas, process-servers or grass-widows.

Nay; we do not bubble with rejoicing when such fruits of psychological deep-down-diving and much-mud-upbringing researches are laid before us, for after all they do not offer us any nourishment, there is nothing in them to engage our teeth, they fail to make life more comprehensible, and hence more bearable. What we yearn to know something about is the process whereby the ideas of everyday are engendered in the skulls of those about us, to the end that we may pursue a straighter and a safer course through the muddle that is life. Why do the great majority of Presbyterians (and, for that matter, of Baptists,

Episcopalians, and Swedenborgians as well) regard it as unlucky to meet a black cat and lucky to find a pin? What are the logical steps behind the theory that it is indecent to eat peas with a knife? By what process does an otherwise sane man arrive at the conclusion that he will go to hell unless he is baptized by total immersion in water? What causes men to be faithful to their wives: habit, fear, poverty, lack of imagination, lack of enterprise, stupidity, religion? What is the psychological basis of commercial morality? What is the true nature of the vague pooling of desires that Rousseau called the social contract? Why does an American regard it as scandalous to wear dress clothes at a funeral, and a Frenchman regard it as equally scandalous *not* to wear them? Why is it that men trust one another so readily, and women trust one another so seldom? Why are we all so greatly affected by statements that we know are not true?—*e. g.* in Lincoln's Gettysburg speech, the Declaration of Independence and the CIII Psalm. What is the origin of the so-called double standard of morality? Why are women forbidden to take off their hats in church? What is happiness? Intelligence? Sin? Courage? Virtue? Beauty?

All these are questions of interest and importance to all of us, for their solution would materially improve the accuracy of our outlook upon the world, and with it our mastery of our environment, but the psychologists, busily engaged in chasing their tails, leave them unanswered, and, in most cases, even unasked. The late William James, more acute than the general, saw how precious little was known about the psychological inwardness of religion, and to the illumination of this darkness he addressed himself in his book, "The Varieties of Religious Experience." But life being short and science long, he got little beyond the statement of the problem and the marshaling of the grosser evidence—and even at this business he allowed himself to be constantly interrupted by spooks, hobgoblins, seventh sons of seventh sons and other such characteristic pets of psychologists. In the same way one Gustav le Bon, a Frenchman, undertook a psychological study of the crowd mind—and then blew up. Add the investigations of Freud and his school, chiefly into abnormal states of mind, and those of Lombroso and his school, chiefly quackish and for the yellow journals, and the idle romancing of such inquirers as Prof. Dr. Thorstein Veblen, and you have exhausted the list of contributions to what may be called practical and everyday psychology. The rev. professors, I daresay, have been doing some useful plowing and planting. All of their meticulous pin-sticking and measuring and chart-making, in the course of time, will enable their successors to approach the real problems of mind with more assurance than is now possible, and perhaps help to their solution. But in the meantime the public and social utility of psychology remains very small, for it is still unable to differentiate accurately between the true and the false, or to give us any effective protection against the fallacies, superstitions, crazes and hysterias which rage in the world.

In this emergency it is not only permissible but even laudable for the amateur to sniff inquiringly through the psychological pasture, essaying modestly to uproot things that the myopic (or, perhaps more accurately, hypermetropic) professionals have overlooked. The late Friedrich Wilhelm Nietzsche did it often, and the usufructs were many curious and daring guesses, some of them probably close to accuracy, as to the genesis of this, that or the other common delusion of man—*i. e.*, the delusion that the law of the survival of the fittest may be repealed by an act of Congress. Into the same field several very interesting expeditions have been made by Dr. Elsie Clews Parsons, a lady once celebrated by Park Row for her invention of trial marriage—an invention, by the way, in which the Nietzsche aforesaid preceded her by at least a dozen years. The records of her researches are to be found in a brief series of books: "The Family," "The Old-Fashioned Woman" and "Fear and Conventionality." Apparently they have wrung relatively little esteem from the learned, for I seldom encounter a reference to them, and Dr. Parsons herself is denied the very modest reward of mention in "Who's Who in America." Nevertheless, they are extremely instructive books, particularly "Fear and Conventionality." I know of no other work, indeed, which offers a better array of observations upon that powerful complex of assumptions, prejudices, instinctive reactions, racial emotions and unbreakable vices of mind which enters so massively into the daily thinking of all of us. The author does not concern herself, as so many psychologists fall into the habit of doing, with thinking as a purely laboratory phenomenon, a process in vacuo. What she deals with is thinking as it is done by men and women in the real world—thinking that is only half intellectual, the other half being as automatic and unintelligent as swallowing, blinking the eye or falling in love.

The power of the complex that I have mentioned is usually very much underestimated, not only by psychologists, but also by all other persons who pretend to culture. We take pride in the fact that we are thinking animals, and like to believe that our thoughts are free, but the truth is that nine-tenths of them are rigidly conditioned by the babbling that goes on around us from birth, and that the business of considering this babbling objectively, separating the true in it from the false, is an intellectual feat of such stupendous difficulty that very few men are ever able to achieve it. The amazing slanging which went on between the English professors and the German professors in the early days of the late war showed how little even cold and academic men are really moved by the bald truth and how much by hot and unintelligible likes and dislikes. The patriotic hysteria of the war simply allowed these eminent pedagogues to say of one another openly and to loud applause what they would have been ashamed to say in times of greater amenity, and what most of them would have denied stoutly that they believed. Nevertheless, it is probably a fact that before there was a sign of war the average English professor, deep down in his heart, thought that any man who ate sauerkraut, and went to the opera in a sackcoat, and intrigued for the appellation of *Geheimrat,* and preferred German music to English poetry, and venerated Bismarck, and called his wife "Mutter," was a scoundrel. He did not say so aloud, and no doubt it would have offended him had you accused him of believing it, but he believed it all the same, and his belief in it gave a muddy, bilious color to his view of German metaphysics, German electro-chemistry and the German chronology of Babylonian kings. And by the same token the average German professor, far down in the ghostly recesses of his hulk, held that any man who read the London *Times,* and ate salt fish at first breakfast, and drank tea of an afternoon, and spoke of Oxford as a university was a *Schafskopf*, a *Schuft* and possibly even a *Schweinehund*.

Nay, not one of us is a free agent. Not one of us actually thinks for himself, or in any orderly and scientific manner. The pressure of environment, of mass ideas, of the socialized intelligence, improperly so called, is too enormous to be withstood. No American, no matter how sharp his critical sense, can ever get away from the notion that democracy is, in some subtle and mysterious way, more conducive to human progress and more pleasing to a just God than any of the systems of government which stand opposed to it. In the privacy of his study he may observe very clearly that it exalts the facile and specious man above the really competent man, and from this observation he may draw the conclusion that its abandonment would be desirable, but once he emerges from his academic seclusion and resumes the rubbing of noses with his fellow-men, he will begin to be tortured by a sneaking feeling that such ideas are heretical and unmanly, and the next time the band begins to play he will thrill with the best of them—or the worst. The actual phenomenon, in truth, was copiously on display during the war. Having myself the character among my acquaintances of one holding the democratic theory in some doubt, I was often approached by gentlemen who told me, in great confidence, that they had been seized by the same tremors. Among them were journalists employed daily in demanding that democracy be forced upon the whole world, and army officers engaged, at least theoretically, in forcing it. All these men, in reflective moments, struggled with ifs and buts. But every one of them, in his public capacity as a good citizen, quickly went back to *thinking* as a good citizen was then expected to think, and even to a certain inflammatory ranting for what, behind the door, he gravely questioned. . . .

It is the business of Dr. Parsons, in "Fear and Conventionality," to prod into certain of the ideas which thus pour into every man's mind from the circumambient air, sweeping away, like some huge cataract, the feeble resistance that his own powers of ratiocination can offer. In particular, she devotes herself to an examination of those general ideas which condition the thought and action of man as a social being —those general ideas which govern his everyday attitude toward his fellow-men and his prevailing view of himself. In one direction they lay upon us the bonds of what we call etiquette, *i. e.*, the duty of considering the habits and feelings of those around us—and in another direction they throttle us with what we call morality—*i. e.*, the rules which protect the life and property of those around us. But, as Dr. Parsons shows, the boundary between etiquette and morality is very dimly drawn, and it is often impossible to say of a given action whether it is downright immoral or merely a breach of the punctilio. Even when the moral law is plainly running, considerations of mere amenity and politeness may still make themselves felt. Thus, as Dr. Parsons points out, there is even an etiquette of adultery. "The *ami de la famille* vows not to kiss his mistress in her husband's house"—not in fear, but "as an expression of conjugal consideration," as a sign that he has not forgotten the thoughtfulness expected of a gentleman. And in this delicate field, as might be expected, the differences in racial attitudes are almost diametrical. The Englishman, surprising his wife with a lover, sues the rogue for damages and has public opinion behind him, but for an American to do it would be for him to lose caste at once and forever. The plain and only duty of the American is to open upon the fellow with artillery, hitting him if the scene is south of the Potomac and missing him if it is above.

I confess to an endless interest in such puzzling niceties, and to much curiosity as to their origins and meaning. Why do we Americans take off our hats when we meet a flapper on the street, and yet stand covered before a male of the highest eminence? A Continental would regard this last as boorish to the last degree; in greeting any equal or superior, male or female, actual or merely conventional, he lifts his

head-piece.   Why does it strike us as ludicrous to see
a man in dress clothes before 6 P. M.?   The Continental puts them on whenever he has a solemn visit to
make, whether the hour be six or noon.   Why do we
regard it as indecent to tuck the napkin between the
waistcoat buttons—or into the neck!—at meals?   The
Frenchman does it without thought of crime.   So does
the Italian.   So does the German.   All three are
punctilious men—far more so, indeed, than we are.
Why do we snicker at the man who wears a wedding
ring?   Most Continentals would stare askance at the
husband who didn't.   Why is it bad manners in Europe and America to ask a stranger his or her age, and
a friendly attention in China?   Why do we regard it
as absurd to distinguish a woman by her husband's
title—e. g., Mrs. Judge Jones, Mrs. Professor Smith?
In Teutonic and Scandinavian Europe the omission of
the title would be looked upon as an affront.

Such fine distinctions, so ardently supported, raise
many interesting questions, but the attempt to answer
them quickly gets one bogged.   Several years ago I
ventured to lift a sad voice against a custom common
in America: that of married men, in speaking of their
wives, employing the full panoply of "Mrs. Brown."
It was my contention—supported, I thought, by logical considerations of the loftiest order—that a husband, in speaking of his wife to his equals, should say
"my wife"—that the more formal mode of designa-

tion should be reserved for inferiors and for strangers of undetermined position. This contention, somewhat to my surprise, was vigorously combated by various volunteer experts. At first they rested their case upon the mere authority of custom, forgetting that this custom was by no means universal. But finally one of them came forward with a more analytical and cogent defense—the defense, to wit, that "my wife" connoted proprietorship and was thus offensive to a wife's *amour propre*. But what of "my sister" and "my mother"? Surely it is nowhere the custom for a man, addressing an equal, to speak of his sister as "Miss Smith." . . . The discussion, however, came to nothing. It was impossible to carry it on logically. The essence of all such inquiries lies in the discovery that there is a force within the liver and lights of man that is infinitely more potent than logic. His reflections, perhaps, may take on intellectually recognizable forms, but they seldom lead to intellectually recognizable conclusions.

Nevertheless, Dr. Parsons offers something in her book that may conceivably help to a better understanding of them, and that is the doctrine that the strange persistence of these rubber-stamp ideas, often unintelligible and sometimes plainly absurd, is due to fear, and that this fear is the product of a very real danger. The safety of human society lies in the assumption that every individual composing it, in a given situation, will act in a manner hitherto approved as seemly. That is to say, he is expected to react to his environment according to a fixed pattern, not necessarily because that pattern is the best imaginable, but simply because it is determined and understood. If he fails to do so, if he reacts in a novel manner—conducive, perhaps, to his better advantage or to what he thinks is his better advantage—then he disappoints the expectation of those around him, and forces them to meet the new situation he has created by the exercise of independent thought. Such independent thought, to a good many men, is quite impossible, and to the overwhelming majority of men, extremely painful. "To all of us," says Dr. Parsons, "to the animal, to the savage and to the civilized being, few demands are as uncomfortable, . . . disquieting or fearful, as the call to innovate. . . . Adaptations we all of us dislike or hate. We dodge or shirk them as best we may." And the man who compels us to make them against our wills we punish by withdrawing from him that understanding and friendliness which he, in turn, looks for and counts upon. In other words, we set him apart as one who is anti-social and not to be dealt with, and according as his rebellion has been small or great, we call him a boor or a criminal.

This distrust of the unknown, this fear of doing something unusual, is probably at the bottom of many ideas and institutions that are commonly credited to other motives. For example, monogamy. The orthodox explanation of monogamy is that it is a manifestation of the desire to have and to hold property—that the husband defends his solitary right to his wife, even at the cost of his own freedom, because she is the pearl among his chattels. But Dr. Parsons argues, and with a good deal of plausibility, that the real moving force, both in the husband and the wife, may be merely the force of habit, the antipathy to experiment and innovation. It is easier and safer to stick to the one wife than to risk adventures with another wife—and the immense social pressure that I have just described is all on the side of sticking. Moreover, the indulgence of a habit automatically strengthens its bonds. What we have done once or thought once, we are more apt than we were before to do and think again. Or, as the late Prof. William James put it, "the selection of a particular hole to live in, of a particular mate, . . . a particular anything, in short, out of a possible multitude . . . carries with it an insensibility to *other* opportunities and occasions—an insensibility which can only be described physiologically as an inhibition of new impulses by the habit of old ones already formed. The possession of homes and wives of our own makes us strangely insensible to the charms of other people. . . . The original impulse which got us homes, wives, . . . seems to exhaust itself in its first achievements and to leave no surplus energy for reacting on new cases." Thus the benedict looks no more on women (at least for a while), and the post-honeymoon bride, as the late David Graham Phillips once told us, neglects the bedizenments which got her a man.

In view of the popular or general character of most of the taboos which put a brake upon personal liberty in thought and action—that is to say, in view of their enforcement by people in the mass, and not by definite specialists in conduct—it is quite natural to find that they are of extra force in democratic societies, for it is the distinguishing mark of democratic societies that they exalt the powers of the majority almost infinitely, and tend to deny the minority any rights whatever. Under a society dominated by a small caste the revolutionist in custom, despite the axiom to the contrary, has a relatively easy time of it, for the persons whose approval he seeks for his innovation are relatively few in number, and most of them are already habituated to more or less intelligible and independent thinking. But under a democracy he is opposed by a horde so vast that it is a practical impossibility for him, without complex and expensive machinery, to reach and convince all of its members, and even if he could reach them he would find most of them quite incapable of rising out of their accustomed grooves. They cannot understand innovations that are genuinely novel and they don't want to understand them; their one desire is to put them down. Even at this late day, with enlightenment raging through the republic like a pestilence, it would cost the average Southern or Middle Western Congressman his seat if he appeared among his constituents in spats, or wearing a wrist-watch. And if a Justice of the Supreme Court of the United States, however gigantic his learning and his juridic rectitude, were taken in crim. con. with the wife of a Senator, he would be destroyed instanter. And if, suddenly revolting against the democratic idea, he were to propose, however gingerly, its abandonment, he would be destroyed with the same dispatch.

But how, then, explain the fact that the populace is constantly ravished and set aflame by fresh brigades of moral, political and sociological revolutionists—that it is forever playing the eager victim to new mountebanks? The explanation lies in the simple circumstance that these performers upon the public midriff are always careful to ladle out nothing actually new, and hence nothing incomprehensible, alarming and accursed. What they offer is always the same old panacea with an extra-gaudy label—the tried, tasted and much-loved dose, the colic cure that mother used to make. Superficially, the United States seems to suffer from an endless and astounding neophilism; actually all its thinking is done within the boundaries of a very small group of political, economic and religious ideas, most of them unsound. For example, there is the fundamental idea of democracy—the idea that all political power should remain in the hands of the populace, that its exercise by superior men is intrinsically immoral. Out of this idea spring innumerable notions and crazes that are no more, at bottom, than restatements of it in sentimental terms: rotation in office, direct elections, the initiative and referendum, the recall, the popular primary, and so on. Again, there is the primary doctrine that the possession of great wealth is a crime—a doctrine half a religious heritage and half the product of mere mob envy. Out of it have come free silver, trust-busting, government ownership, muck-raking, Populism, Bleaseism, Progressivism, the milder forms of Socialism, the whole gasconade of "reform" politics. Yet again, there is the ineradicable peasant suspicion of the man who is having a better time in the world—a suspicion grounded, like the foregoing, partly upon undisguised envy and partly upon archaic and barbaric religious taboos. Out of it have come all the glittering pearls of the uplift, from Abolition to Prohibition, and from the crusade against horse-racing to the Mann Act. The whole political history of the United States is a history of these three ideas. There has never been an issue before the people that could not be translated into one or another of them. What is more, they have also colored the fundamental philosophical (and particularly epistemological) doctrines of the American people, and their moral theory, and even their foreign relations. The late war, very unpopular at the start, was "sold" to them, as the advertising phrase has it, by representing it as a campaign for the salvation of democracy, half religious and wholly altruistic. So represented to them, they embraced it; represented as the highly obscure and complex thing it actually was, it would have been beyond their comprehension, and hence abhorrent to them.

Outside this circle of their elemental convictions they are quite incapable of rational thought. One is not surprised to hear of Bismarck, a thorough royalist, discussing democracy with calm and fairness, but it would be unimaginable for the American people, or for any other democratic people, to discuss royalism in the same manner: it would take a cataclysm to bring them to any such violation of their mental habits. When such a cataclysm occurs, they embrace the new ideas that are its fruits with the same adamantine firmness. One year before the French Revolution, disobedience to the king was unthinkable to the average Frenchman; only a few daringly immoral men cherished the notion. But one year *after* the fall of the Bastile, obedience to the king was equally unthinkable. The Russian Bolsheviki, whose doings have furnished a great deal of immensely interesting material to the student of popular psychology, put the principle into plain words. Once they were in the saddle, they decreed the abolition of the old imperial censorship and announced that speech would be free henceforth—but only so long as it kept within the bounds of the Bolshevist revelation! In other words, any citizen was free to think and speak whatever he pleased—but only so long as it did not violate certain fundamental ideas. This is precisely the sort of freedom that has prevailed in the United States since the first days. It is the only sort of freedom comprehensible to the average man. It accurately reveals his constitutional inability to shake himself free from the illogical and often quite unintelligible prejudices, instincts and mental vices that condition ninety per cent. of all his thinking. . . .

But here I wander into political speculation and no doubt stand in contumacy of some statute of Congress. Dr. Parsons avoids politics in her very interesting book. She confines herself to the purely social relations, *e. g.*, between man and woman, parent and child, host and guest, master and servant. The facts she offers are vastly interesting, and their discovery and coördination reveal a tremendous industry, but of even greater interest are the facts that lie over the margin of her inquiry. Here is a golden opportunity for other investigators: I often wonder that the field is so little explored. Perhaps the Freudians,

once they get rid of their sexual obsession, will enter
it and chart it.   No doubt the inferiority complex described by Prof. Dr. Alfred Adler will one day pro-
vide an intelligible explanation of many of the puzzling phenomena of mob thinking.   In the work of
Prof. Dr. Freud himself there is, perhaps, a clew to
the origin and anatomy of Puritanism, that worst of
intellectual nephritises.   I live in hope that the Freudians will fall upon the business without much further
delay.   Why do otherwise sane men believe in spirits?
What is the genesis of the American axiom that the
fine arts are unmanly?   What is the precise machinery of the process called falling in love?   Why do
people believe newspapers? . . . Let there be light!

XIII. THE AMERICAN MAGAZINE

IT is astonishing, considering the enormous influence of the popular magazine upon American literature, such as it is, that there is but one book in type upon magazine history in the republic. That lone volume is "The Magazine in America," by Prof. Dr. Algernon Tassin, a learned birchman of the great university of Columbia, and it is so badly written that the interest of its matter is almost concealed—almost, but fortunately not quite. The professor, in fact, puts English to paper with all the traditional dullness of his flatulent order, and, as usual, he is most horribly dull when he is trying most kittenishly to be lively. I spare you examples of his writing; if you know the lady essayists of the United States, and their academic imitators in pantaloons, you know the sort of arch and whimsical jocosity he ladles out. But, as I have hinted, there is something worth attending to in his story, for all the defects of its presentation, and so his book is not to be sniffed at. He has, at all events, brought together a great mass of scattered and concealed facts, and arranged them conveniently for whoever deals with them next. The job was plainly a long and laborious one, and rasping to the higher cerebral centers. The historian had to make his mole-like way through the endless files of old and stupid magazines; he had to read the insipid biographies and autobiographies of dead and forgotten editors, many of them college professors, preachers out of work, pre-historic uplifters and bad poets; he had to sort out the facts from the fancies of such incurable liars as Griswold; he had to hack and blast a path across a virgin wilderness. The thing was worth doing, and, as I say, it has been done with commendable pertinacity.

Considering the noisiness of the American magazines of to-day, it is rather instructive to glance back at the timorous and bloodless quality of their progenitors. All of the early ones, when they were not simply monthly newspapers or almanacs, were depressingly "literary" in tone, and dealt chiefly in stupid poetry, silly essays and artificial fiction. The one great fear of their editors seems to have been that of offending some one; all of the pioneer prospectuses were full of assurances that nothing would be printed which even "the most fastidious" could object to. Literature, in those days,—say from 1830 to 1860—was almost completely cut off from contemporary life. It mirrored, not the struggle for existence, so fierce and dramatic in the new nation, but the pallid reflections of poetasters, self-advertising clergymen, sissified "gentlemen of taste," and other such donkeys. Poe waded into these *literati* and shook them up a bit, but even after the Civil War the majority of them continued to spin pretty cobwebs. Edmund Clarence Stedman and Donald G. Mitchell were excellent specimens of the clan; its last survivor was the lachrymose William Winter. The "literature" manufactured by these tear-squeezers, though often enough produced in beer cellars, was frankly aimed at the Young Person. Its main purpose was to avoid giving offense; it breathed a heavy and oleaginous piety, a snug niceness, a sickening sweetness. It is as dead to-day as Baalam's ass.

The *Atlantic Monthly* was set up by men in revolt against this reign of mush, as *Putnam's* had been a few years before, but the business of reform proved to be difficult and hazardous, and it was a long while before a healthier breed of authors could be developed, and a public for them found. "There is not much in the *Atlantic*," wrote Charles Eliot Norton to Lowell in 1874, "that is likely to be read twice save by its writers, and this is what the great public likes. . . . You should hear Godkin express himself in private on this topic." *Harper's Magazine*, in those days, was made up almost wholly of cribbings from England; the *North American Review* had sunk into stodginess and imbecility; *Putnam's* was dead, or dying; the *Atlantic* had yet to discover Mark Twain; it was the era of *Godey's Lady's Book.* The new note, so long awaited, was struck at last by *Scribner's,* now the *Century* (and not to be confused with the *Scribner's* of to-day). It not only threw all the old traditions overboard; it established new traditions almost at once. For the first time a great magazine began to take notice of the daily life of the American people. It started off with a truly remarkable series of articles on the Civil War; it plunged into contemporary politics; it eagerly sought out and encouraged new writers; it began printing decent pictures instead of the old chromos; it forced itself, by the sheer originality and enterprise of its editing, upon the public attention. American literature owes more to the *Century* than to any other magazine, and perhaps American thinking owes almost as much. It was the first "literary" periodical to arrest and interest the really first-class men of the country. It beat the *Atlantic* because it wasn't burdened with the *Atlantic's* decaying cargo of Boston Brahmins. It beat all the others because it was infinitely and obviously better. Almost everything that is good in the American magazine of to-day, almost everything that sets it above the English magazine or the Continental magazine, stems from the *Century.*

At the moment, of course, it holds no such clear field; perhaps it has served its function and is ready for a placid old age. The thing that displaced it was

the yellow magazine of the *McClure's* type—a variety
of magazine which surpassed it in the race for circulation by exaggerating and vulgarizing all its merits.   Dr. Tassin seems to think, with William Archer,
that S. S. McClure was the inventor of this type, but
the truth is that its real father was the unknown orig-
inator of the Sunday supplement.   What McClure
—a shrewd literary bagman—did was to apply the
sensational methods of the cheap newspaper to a new
and cheap magazine.   Yellow journalism was rising
and he went in on the tide.   The satanic Hearst was
getting on his legs at the same time, and I daresay
that the muck-raking magazines, even in their palmy
days, followed him a good deal more than they led
him.   McClure and the imitators of McClure borrowed his adept thumping of the tom-tom; Munsey
and the imitators of Munsey borrowed his mush.
McClure's and *Everybody's*, even when they had the
whole nation by the ears, did little save repeat in
solemn, awful tones what Hearst had said before.
As for *Munsey's*, at the height of its circulation, it was
little more than a Sunday "magazine section" on
smooth paper, and with somewhat clearer half-tones
than Hearst could print.   Nearly all the genuinely
original ideas of these Yankee Harmsworths of yesterday turned out badly.   John Brisben Walker, with
the *Cosmopolitan*, tried to make his magazine a sort
of national university, and it went to pot.   Ridgway,

of *Everybody's,* planned a weekly to be published in
a dozen cities simultaneously, and lost a fortune trying to establish it. McClure, facing a situation to
be described presently, couldn't manage it, and his
magazine got away from him. As for Munsey, there
are many wrecks behind him; he is forever experi-
menting boldly and failing gloriously. Even his
claim to have invented the all-fiction magazine is open
to caveat; there were probably plenty of such things,
in substance if not in name, before the *Argosy.*
Hearst, the teacher of them all, now openly holds the
place that belongs to him. He has galvanized the
corpse of the old *Cosmopolitan* into a great success, he
has distanced all rivals with *Hearst's,* he has beaten
the English on their own ground with *Nash's,* and he
has rehabilitated various lesser magazines. More,
he has forced the other magazine publishers to imitate him. A glance at *McClure's* to-day offers all the
proof that is needed of his influence upon his inferiors.

Dr. Tassin, apparently in fear of making his book
too nearly good, halts his chronicle at its most interesting point, for he says nothing of what has gone on
since 1900—and very much, indeed, has gone on
since 1900. For one thing, the *Saturday Evening
Post* has made its unparalleled success, created its new
type of American literature for department store buy-
ers and shoe drummers, and bred its school of brisk,

business-like, high-speed authors. For another thing, the *Ladies' Home Journal,* once supreme in its field, has seen the rise of a swarm of imitators, some of them very prosperous. For a third thing, the all-fiction magazine of Munsey, Robert Bonner and Street & Smith has degenerated into so dubious a hussy that Munsey, a very moral man, must blush every time he thinks of it. For a fourth thing, the moving-picture craze has created an entirely new type of magazine, and it has elbowed many other types from the stands. And for a fifth thing, to make an end, the muck-raking magazine has blown up and is no more.

Why this last? Have all the possible candidates for the rake been raked? Is there no longer any taste for scandal in the popular breast? I have heard endless discussion of these questions and many ingenious answers, but all of them fail to answer. In this emergency I offer one of my own. It is this: that the muck-raking magazine came to grief, not because the public tired of muck-raking, but because the muck-raking that it began with succeeded. That is to say, the villains so long belabored by the Steffenses, the Tarbells and the Phillipses were either driven from the national scene or forced (at least temporarily) into rectitude. Worse, their places in public life were largely taken by nominees whose chemical purity was guaranteed by these same magazines, and so the latter found their occupation gone and their following with it.   The great masses of the plain people, eager to swallow denunciation in horse-doctor doses, gagged at the first spoonful of praise.   They chortled and read on when Aldrich, Boss Cox, Gas Addicks, John D. Rockefeller and the other bugaboos of the time were belabored every month, but they promptly sickened and went elsewhere when Judge Ben B. Lindsey, Francis J. Heney, Governor Folk and the rest of the bogus saints began to be hymned.

The same phenomenon is constantly witnessed upon the lower level of daily journalism.   Let a vociferous "reform" newspaper overthrow the old gang and elect its own candidates, and at once it is in a perilous condition.   Its stock in trade is gone.   It can no longer give a good show—within the popular meaning of a good show.   For what the public wants eternally— at least the American public—is rough work.   It delights in vituperation.   It revels in scandal.   It is always on the side of the man or journal making the charges, no matter how slight the probability that the accused is guilty.   The late Roosevelt, perhaps one of the greatest rabble-rousers the world has ever seen, was privy to this fact, and made it the corner-stone of his singularly cynical and effective politics.   He was forever calling names, making accusations, unearthing and denouncing demons.   Dr. Wilson, a performer of scarcely less talent, has sought to pursue the same plan, with varying fidelity and success.   He was a popular hero so long as he confined himself to reviling men and things—the Hell Hounds of Plutocracy, the Socialists, the Kaiser, the Irish, the Senate minority. But the moment he found himself on the side of the defense, he began to wobble, just as Roosevelt before him had begun to wobble when he found himself burdened with the intricate constructive program of the Progressives. Roosevelt shook himself free by deserting the Progressives, but Wilson found it impossible to get rid of his League of Nations, and so, for awhile at least, he presented a quite typical picture of a muck-raker ham-strung by blows from the wrong end of the rake.

That the old appetite for bloody shows is not dead but only sleepeth is well exhibited by the recent revival of the weekly of opinion. Ten years ago the weekly seemed to be absolutely extinct; even the *Nation* survived only as a half-forgotten appendage of the *Evening Post*. Then, of a sudden, the alliance was broken, the *Evening Post* succumbed to Wall Street, the *Nation* started on an independent course— and straightway made a great success. And why? Simply because it began breaking heads—not the old heads of the *McClure's* era, of course, but nevertheless heads salient enough to make excellent targets. For years it had been moribund; no one read it save a dwindling company of old men; its influence gradually approached *nil*. But by the elementary device of

switching from mild expostulation to violent and effective denunciation it made a new public almost
over-night, and is now very widely read, extensively
quoted and increasingly heeded. . . . I often wonder
that so few publishers of periodicals seem aware of
the psychological principle here exposed. It is
known to every newspaper publisher of the slightest
professional intelligence; all successful newspapers
are ceaselessly querulous and bellicose. They never
defend any one or anything if they can help it; if the
job is forced upon them, they tackle it by denouncing
some one or something else. The plan never fails.
Turn to the moving-picture trade magazines: the most
prosperous of them is given over, in the main, to bitter
attacks upon new films. Come back to daily journalism. The New York *Tribune,* a decaying paper, well
nigh rehabilitated itself by attacking Hearst, the clev-
erest muck-raker of them all. For a moment, apparently dismayed, he attempted a defense of himself—and came near falling into actual disaster.
Then, recovering his old form, he began a whole series
of counter attacks and cover attacks, and in six months
he was safe and sound again. . . .

XIV. THE ULSTER POLONIUS

A GOOD half of the humor of the late Mark
Twain consisted of admitting frankly the
possession of vices and weaknesses that all
of us have and few of us care to acknowledge. Practically all of the sagacity of George Bernard Shaw
consists of bellowing vociferously what every one
knows. I think I am as well acquainted with his
works, both hortatory and dramatic, as the next man.
I wrote the first book ever devoted to a discussion of
them, and I read them pretty steadily, even to-day,
and with endless enjoyment. Yet, so far as I know,
I have never found an original idea in them—never a
single statement of fact or opinion that was not an-
teriorly familiar, and almost commonplace. Put the
thesis of any of his plays into a plain proposition, and
I doubt that you could find a literate man in Christendom who had not heard it before, or who would seriously dispute it. The roots of each one of them are
in platitude; the roots of *every* effective stage-play
are in platitude; that a dramatist is inevitably a platitudinarian is itself a platitude double damned. But
Shaw clings to the obvious even when he is not ham-
pered by the suffocating conventions of the stage.

His Fabian tracts and his pamphlets on the war are veritable compendiums of the undeniable; what is seriously stated in them is quite beyond logical dispute. They have excited a great deal of ire, they have brought down upon him a great deal of amusing abuse, but I have yet to hear of any one actually controverting them. As well try to controvert the Copernican astronomy. They are as bullet-proof in essence as the multiplication table, and vastly more bullet-proof than the Ten Commandments or the Constitution of the United States.

Well, then, why does the Ulsterman kick up such a pother? Why is he regarded as an arch-heretic, almost comparable to Galileo, Nietzsche or Simon Magnus? For the simplest of reasons. Because he practices with great zest and skill the fine art of exhibiting the obvious in unexpected and terrifying lights—because he is a master of the logical trick of so matching two apparently safe premises that they yield an incongruous and inconvenient conclusion— above all, because he is a fellow of the utmost charm and address, quick-witted, bold, limber-tongued, persuasive, humorous, iconoclastic, ingratiating—in brief, a true Kelt, and so the exact antithesis of the solemn Sassenachs who ordinarily instruct and exhort us. Turn to his "Man and Superman," and you will see the whole Shaw machine at work. What he starts out with is the self-evident fact, disputed by no one not idiotic, that a woman has vastly more to gain by marriage, under Christian monogamy, than a man. That fact is as old as monogamy itself; it was, I daresay, the admitted basis of the palace revolution which brought monogamy into the world. But now comes Shaw with an implication that the sentimentality of the world chooses to conceal—with a deduction plainly resident in the original proposition, but kept in safe silence there by a preposterous and hypocritical taboo—to wit, the deduction that women are well aware of the profit that marriage yields for them, and that they are thus much more eager to marry than men are, and ever alert to take the lead in the business. This second fact, to any man who has passed through the terrible years between twenty-five and forty, is as plain as the first, but by a sort of general consent it is not openly stated. Violate that general consent and you are guilty of *scandalum magnatum.* Shaw is simply one who is guilty of *scandalum magnatum* habitually, a professional criminal in that department. It is his life work to announce the obvious in terms of the scandalous.

What lies under the horror of such blabbing is the deepest and most widespread of human weaknesses, which is to say, intellectual cowardice, the craven appetite for mental ease and security, the fear of thinking things out. All men are afflicted by it more or less; not even the most courageous and frank of

men likes to admit, in specific terms, that his wife is
fat, or that she seduced him to the altar by a trans-
parent trick, or that their joint progeny resemble her
brother or father, and are thus cads. A few extraordinary heroes of logic and evidence may do it
occasionally, but only occasionally. The average
man never does it at all. He is eternally in fear of
what he knows in his heart; his whole life is made up
of efforts to dodge it and conceal it; he is always running away from what passes for his intelligence and
taking refuge in what pass for his higher feelings, *i. e.,*
his stupidities, his delusions, his sentimentalities.
Shaw is devoted to the art of hauling this recreant
fellow up. He is one who, for purposes of sensation,
often for the mere joy of outraging the tender-
minded, resolutely and mercilessly thinks things out
—sometimes with the utmost ingenuity and humor,
but often, it must be said, in the same muddled way
that the average right-thinker would do it if he ever
got up the courage. Remember this formula, and
all of the fellow's alleged originality becomes no more
than a sort of bad-boy audacity, usually in bad taste.
He drags skeletons from their closet and makes them
dance obscenely—but every one, of course, knew that
they were there all the while. He would produce an
excitement of exactly the same kind (though perhaps
superior in intensity) if he should walk down the
Strand bared to the waist, and so remind the shocked

Londoners of the unquestioned fact (though conventionally concealed and forgotten) that he is a mammal, and has an umbilicus.

Turn to a typical play-and-preface of his later canon, say "Androcles and the Lion." Here the complete Shaw formula is exposed. On the one hand there is a mass of platitudes; on the other hand there is the air of a peep-show. On the one hand he rehearses facts so stale that even Methodist clergymen have probably heard of them; on the other hand he states them so scandalously that the pious get all of the thrills out of the business that would accompany a view of the rector in liquor in the pulpit. Here, for example, are some of his contentions:

(a) That the social and economic doctrines preached by Jesus were indistinguishable from what is now called Socialism.

(b) That the Pauline transcendentalism visible in the Acts and the Epistles differs enormously from the simple humanitarianism set forth in the Four Gospels.

(c) That the Christianity on tap to-day would be almost as abhorrent to Jesus, supposing Him returned to earth, as the theories of Nietzsche, Hindenburg or Clemenceau, and vastly more abhorrent than those of Emma Goldman.

(d) That the rejection of the Biblical miracles, and even of the historical credibility of the Gospels, by no means disposes of Christ Himself.

(e) That the early Christians were persecuted, not because their theology was regarded as unsound, but because their public conduct constituted a nuisance.

It is unnecessary to go on.   Could any one imagine
a more abject surrender to the undeniable?   Would
it be possible to reduce the German exegesis of a century and a half to a more depressing series of platitudes?   But his discussion of the inconsistencies
between the Four Gospels is even worse; you will
find all of its points set forth in any elemental treatise
upon New Testament criticism—even in so childish a
tract as Ramsden Balmforth's.   He actually dishes
up, with a heavy air of profundity, the news that there
is a glaring conflict between the genealogy of Jesus in
Matthew i, 1–17, and the direct claim of divine
paternity in Matthew i, 18.   More, he breaks out
with the astounding discovery that Jesus was a good
Jew, and that Paul's repudiation of circumcision
(now a cardinal article of the so-called Christian
faith) would have surprised Him and perhaps greatly
shocked Him.   The whole preface, running to 114
pages, is made up of just such shop-worn stuff.
Searching it from end to end with eagle eye, I have
failed to find a single fact or argument that was not
previously familiar to me, despite the circumstance
that I ordinarily give little attention to the sacred
sciences and thus might have been expected to be surprised by their veriest commonplaces.

Nevertheless, this preface makes bouncing reading
—and therein lies the secret of the continued vogue of
Shaw.   He has a large and extremely uncommon

capacity for provocative utterance; he knows how to get a touch of bellicosity into the most banal of doctrines; he is forever on tiptoe, forever challenging, forever *sforzando*. His matter may be from the public store, even from the public junk-shop, but his manner is always all his own. The tune is old, but the words are new. Consider, for example, his discussion of the personality of Jesus. The idea is simple and obvious: Jesus was not a long-faced prophet of evil, like John the Baptist, nor was He an ascetic, or a mystic. But here is the Shaw way of saying it: "He was . . . what we call an artist and a Bohemian in His manner of life." The fact remains unchanged, but in the extravagant statement of it there is a shock for those who have been confusing the sour donkey they hear of a Sunday with the tolerant, likable Man they profess to worship—and perhaps there is even a genial snicker in it for their betters. So with his treatment of the Atonement. His objections to it are time-worn, but suddenly he gets the effect of novelty by pointing out the quite manifest fact that acceptance of it is apt to make for weakness, that the man who rejects it is thrown back upon his own courage and circumspection, and is hence stimulated to augment them. The first argument—that Jesus was of free and easy habits—is so commonplace that I have heard it voiced by a bishop. The second suggests itself so naturally that I myself

once employed it against a chance Christian encountered in a Pullman smoking-room. This Christian was at first shocked as he might have been by
reading Shaw, but in half an hour he was confessing
that he had long ago thought of the objection himself,
and put it away as immoral. I well remember his
fascinated interest as I showed him how my inability
to accept the doctrine put a heavy burden of moral
responsibility upon me, and forced me to be more
watchful of my conduct than the elect of God, and
so robbed me of many pleasant advantages in finance,
the dialectic and amour. . . .

A double jest conceals itself in the Shaw legend.
The first half of it I have already disclosed. The
second half has to do with the fact that Shaw is not
at all the wholesale agnostic his fascinated victims
see him, but an orthodox Scotch Presbyterian of the
most cock-sure and bilious sort—in fact, almost the
archetype of the blue-nose. In the theory that he is
Irish I take little stock. His very name is as Scotch
as haggis, and the part of Ireland from which he
springs is peopled almost exclusively by Scots. The
true Irishman is a romantic. He senses life as a
mystery, a thing of wonder, an experience of passion
and beauty. In politics he is not logical, but emotional. In religion his interest centers, not in the
commandments, but in the sacraments. The Scot, on
the contrary, is almost devoid of romanticism. He

is a materialist, a logician, a utilitarian.   Life to him
is not a poem, but a series of police regulations.
God is not an indulgent father, but a hanging judge.
There are no saints, but only devils.   Beauty is a
lewdness, redeemable only in the service of morality.
It is more important to get on in the world than to be
brushed by angels' wings.   Here Shaw runs exactly
true to type.   Read his critical writings from end to
end, and you will not find the slightest hint that
objects of art were passing before him as he wrote.
He founded, in England, the superstition that Ibsen
was no more than a tin-pot evangelist—a sort of
brother to General Booth, Mrs. Pankhurst and the
syndics of the Sex Hygiene Society.   He turned
Shakespeare into a bird of evil, croaking dismally
in a rain-barrel.   He even injected a moral content
(by dint of herculean straining) into the music
dramas of Richard Wagner—surely the most colossal
sacrifices of moral ideas ever made on the altar of
beauty!   Always the ethical obsession, the hall-mark
of the Scotch Puritan, is visible in him.   His politics
is mere moral indignation.   His æsthetic theory is
cannibalism upon æsthetics.   And in his general
writing he is forever discovering an atrocity in what
was hitherto passed as no more than a human weakness; he is forever inventing new sins, and demanding
their punishment; he always sees his opponent, not
only as wrong, but also as a scoundrel.   I have called

him a Presbyterian. Need I add that he flirts with
predestination under the quasi-scientific *nom de guerre*
of determinism—that he seems to be convinced that,
while men may not be responsible for their virtues,
they are undoubtedly responsible for their offendings,
and deserve to be clubbed therefor? . . .

And this is Shaw the revolutionist, the heretic!
Next, perhaps, we shall be hearing of Benedict XV,
the atheist. . . .

XV. AN UNHEEDED LAW-GIVER

ONE discerns, in all right-thinking American criticism, the doctrine that Ralph Waldo Emerson was a great man, but the specifications supporting that doctrine are seldom displayed with any clarity. Despite the vast mass of writing about him, he remains to be worked out critically; practically all the existing criticism of him is marked by his own mellifluous obscurity. Perhaps a good deal of this obscurity is due to contradictions inherent in the man's character. He was dualism ambulant. What he actually *was* was seldom identical with what he represented himself to be or what his admirers thought him to be. Universally greeted, in his own day, as a revolutionary, he was, in point of fact, imitative and cautious—an importer of stale German elixirs, sometimes direct and sometimes through the Carlylean branch house, who took good care to dilute them with buttermilk before merchanting them. The theoretical spokesman, all his life long, of bold and forthright thinking, of the unafraid statement of ideas, he stated his own so warily and so muggily that they were ratified on the one hand by Nietzsche and on the other hand by the messiahs of the New Thought, that lavender buncombe.

What one notices about him chiefly is his lack of influence upon the main stream of American thought, such as it is. He had admirers and even worshipers, but no apprentices. Nietzscheism and the New Thought are alike tremendous violations of orthodox American doctrine. The one makes a headlong attack upon egalitarianism, the corner-stone of American politics; the other substitutes mysticism, which is the notion that the true realities are all concealed, for the prevailing American notion that the only true realities lie upon the surface, and are easily discerned by Congressmen, newspaper editorial writers and members of the Junior Order of United American Mechanics. The Emerson cult, in America, has been an affectation from the start. Not many of the chautauqua orators, literary professors, vassarized old maids and other such bogus *intelligentsia* who devote themselves to it have any intelligible understanding of the Transcendentalism at the heart of it, and not one of them, so far as I can make out, has ever executed Emerson's command to "defer never to the popular cry." On the contrary, it is precisely within the circle of Emersonian adulation that one finds the greatest tendency to test all ideas by their respectability, to combat free thought as something intrinsically vicious, and to yield placidly to "some great

decorum, some fetish of a government, some ephem-
eral trade, or war, or man." It is surely not
unworthy of notice that the country of this prophet
of Man Thinking is precisely the country in which
every sort of dissent from the current pishposh is
combated most ferociously, and in which there is the
most vigorous existing tendency to suppress free
speech altogether.

Thus Emerson, on the side of ideas, has left but
faint tracks behind him. His quest was for "facts
amidst appearances," and his whole metaphysic re-
volved around a doctrine of transcendental first
causes, a conception of interior and immutable realities, distinct from and superior to mere transient
phenomena. But the philosophy that actually pre-
vails among his countrymen—a philosophy put into
caressing terms by William James—teaches an almost
exactly contrary doctrine: its central idea is that
whatever satisfies the immediate need is substantially
true, that appearance is the only form of fact worthy
the consideration of a man with money in the bank,
and the old flag floating over him, and hair on his
chest. Nor has Emerson had any ponderable influence as a literary artist in the technical sense, or as
the prophet of a culture—that is, at home. Despite
the feeble imitations of campus critics, his manner
has vanished with his matter. There is, in the true
sense, no Emersonian school of American writers.

Current American writing, with its cocksureness, its somewhat hard competence, its air of selling goods, is utterly at war with his loose, impressionistic method, his often mystifying groping for ideas, his relentless pursuit of phrases.   In the same way, one searches the country in vain for any general reaction to the cultural ideal that he set up.   When one casts about for salient men whom he moved profoundly, men who got light from his torch, one thinks first and last, not of Americans, but of such men as Nietzsche and Hermann Grimm, the Germans, and Tyndall and Matthew Arnold, the Englishmen.   What remains of him at home, as I have said, is no more than, on the one hand, a somewhat absurd affectation of intellectual fastidiousness, now almost extinct even in New England, and, on the other hand, a debased Transcendentalism rolled into pills for fat women with vague pains and inattentive husbands—in brief, the New Thought—in brief, imbecility. This New Thought, a decadent end-product of American superficiality, now almost monopolizes him.   One hears of him in its preposterous literature and one hears of him in text-books for the young, but not often elsewhere.   Allowing everything, it would surely be absurd to hold that he has colored and conditioned the main stream of American thought as Goethe colored and conditioned the thought of Germany, or Pushkin that of Russia, or Voltaire that of France. . . .

XVI. THE BLUSHFUL MYSTERY

1

Sex Hygiene

THE literature of sex hygiene, once so scanty and so timorous, now piles mountain high. There are at least a dozen formidable series of books of instruction for inquirers of all ages, beginning with "What Every Child of Ten Should Know" and ending with "What a Woman of Forty-five Should Know," and they all sell amazingly. Scores of diligent authors, some medical, some clerical and some merely shrewdly chautauqual, grow rich at the industry of composing them. One of these amateur Havelock Ellises had the honor, during the last century, of instructing me in the elements of the sacred sciences. He was then the pastor of a fourth-rate church in a decaying neighborhood and I was sent to his Sunday-school in response to some obscure notion that the agony of it would improve me. Presently he disappeared, and for a long while I heard nothing about him. Then he came into sudden prominence as the author of such a series of handbooks and as the chief stockholder, it would seem, in the publishing house printing them. By the time he died, a few years ago, he had been so well rewarded by a just God that he was able to leave funds to establish a missionary college in some remote and heathen land.

This holy man, I believe, was honest, and took his platitudinous compositions quite seriously. Regarding other contributors to the literature it may be said without malice that their altruism is obviously corrupted by a good deal of hocus-pocus. Some of them lecture in the chautauquas, peddling their books before and after charming the yokels. Others, being members of the faculty, seem to carry on medical practice on the side. Yet others are kept in profitable jobs by the salacious old men who finance vice crusades. It is hard to draw the line between the mere thrifty· enthusiast and the downright fraud. So, too, with the actual vice crusaders. The books of the latter, like the sex hygiene books, are often sold, not as wisdom, but as pornography. True enough, they are always displayed in the show-window of the small-town Methodist Book Concern— but you will also find them in the back-rooms of dubious second-hand book-stores, side by side with the familiar scarlet-backed editions of Rabelais, Margaret of Navarre and Balzac's "Droll Tales." Some time ago, in a book advertisement headed "Snappy Fiction," I found announcements of "My Battles With Vice," by Virginia Brooks—and "Life of My Heart," by Victoria Cross. The former was described by the publisher as a record of "personal experiences in the fight against the gray wolves and love pirates of modern society." The book was offered to all comers by mail. One may easily imagine the effects of such an offer.

But even the most serious and honest of the sex hygiene volumes are probably futile, for they are all founded upon a pedagogical error. That is to say, they are all founded upon an attempt to explain a romantic mystery in terms of an exact science. Nothing could be more absurd: as well attempt to interpret Beethoven in terms of mathematical physics—as many a fatuous contrapuntist, indeed, has tried to do. The mystery of sex presents itself to the young, not as a scientific problem to be solved, but as a romantic emotion to be accounted for. The only result of the current endeavor to explain its phenomena by seeking parallels in botany is to make botany obscene. . . .

2

Art and Sex

One of the favorite notions of the Puritan mullahs who specialize in this moral pornography is that the sex instinct, if suitably repressed, may be "sublimated" into the higher sorts of idealism, and especially into aesthetic idealism. That notion is to be found in all their books; upon it they ground the theory that the enforcement of chastity by a huge force of spies, stool pigeons and police would convert the republic into a nation of incomparable uplifters, forward-lookers and artists. All this, of course, is simply pious fudge. If the notion were actually sound, then all the great artists of the world would come from the ranks of the hermetically repressed, *i. e.,* from the ranks of Puritan old maids, male and female. But the truth is, as every one knows, that the great artists of the world are never Puritans, and seldom even ordinarily respectable. No virtuous man—that is, virtuous in the Y. M. C. A. sense— has ever painted a picture worth looking at, or written a symphony worth hearing, or a book worth reading, and it is highly improbable that the thing has ever been done by a virtuous woman. The actual effect of repression, lamentable though it may be, is to destroy idealism altogether. The Puritan, for all his pretensions, is the worst of materialists. Passed through his sordid and unimaginative mind, even the stupendous romance of sex is reduced to a disgusting transaction in physiology. As artist he is thus hopeless; as well expect an auctioneer to qualify for the Sistine Chapel choir. All he ever achieves, taking pen or brush in hand, is a feeble burlesque of his betters, all of whom, by his hog's theology, are doomed to hell.

3

A Loss to Romance

Perhaps the worst thing that this sex hygiene nonsense has accomplished is the thing mourned by
Agnes Repplier in "The Repeal of Reticence." In
America, at least, innocence has been killed, and
romance has been sadly wounded by the same discharge of smutty artillery. The flapper is no longer
naïve and charming; she goes to the altar of God with
a learned and even cynical glitter in her eye. The
veriest school-girl of to-day, fed upon Forel, Sylvanus
Stall, Reginald Wright Kauffman and the Freud
books, knows as much as the midwife of 1885, and
spends a good deal more time discharging and dis-
seminating her information. All this, of course, is
highly embarrassing to the more romantic and ingenuous sort of men, of whom I have the honor to be
one. We are constantly in the position of General
Mitchener in Shaw's one-acter, "Press Cuttings,"
when he begs Mrs. Farrell, the talkative charwoman,
to reserve her confidences for her medical adviser.
One often wonders, indeed, what women now talk of
to doctors. . . .

Please do not misunderstand me here. I do not
object to this New Freedom on moral grounds, but on
æsthetic grounds. In the relations between the sexes

all beauty is founded upon romance, all romance is founded upon mystery, and all mystery is founded upon ignorance, or, failing that, upon the deliberate denial of the known truth. To be in love is merely to be in a state of perceptual anæsthesia—to mistake an ordinary young man for a Greek god or an ordinary young woman for a goddess. But how can this condition of mind survive the deadly matter-of-factness which sex hygiene and the new science of eugenics impose? How can a woman continue to believe in the honor, courage and loving tenderness of a man after she has learned, perhaps by affidavit, that his hæmoglobin count is 117%, that he is free from sugar and albumen, that his blood pressure is 112/79 and that his Wassermann reaction is negative? . . . Moreover, all this new-fangled "frankness" tends to dam up, at least for civilized adults, one of the principal well-springs of art, to wit, impropriety. What is neither hidden nor forbidden is seldom very charming. If women, continuing their present tendency to its logical goal, end by going stark naked, there will be no more poets and painters, but only dermatologists and photographers. . . .

4

Sex on the Stage

The effort to convert the theater into a forum of solemn sex discussion is another abhorrent by-product of the sex hygiene rumble-bumble. Fortunately, it seems to be failing. A few years ago, crowds flocked to see Brieux's "Les Avariés," but to-day it is forgotten, and its successors are all obscure. The movement originated in Germany with the production of Frank Wedekind's "Frühlings Erwachen." The Germans gaped and twisted in their seats for a season or two, and then abandoned sex as a horror and went back to sex as a comedy. This last is what it actually should be, at least in the theater. The theater is no place for painful speculation; it is a place for diverting representation. Its best and truest sex plays are not such overstrained shockers as "Le Mariage d' Olympe" and "Damaged Goods," but such penetrating and excellent comedies as "Much Ado About Nothing" and "The Taming of the Shrew." In "Much Ado" we have an accurate and unforgettable picture of the way in which the normal male of the human species is brought to the altar—that is, by the way of appealing to his hollow vanity, the way of capitalizing his native and ineradicable asininity. And in "The Taming of the Shrew" we have a picture of the way in which the average woman, having so snared him, is purged of her resultant vainglory and bombast, and thus reduced to decent discipline and decorum, that the marriage may go on in solid tranquillity.

The whole drama of sex, in real life, as well as on

the stage, revolves around these two enterprises.
One-half of it consists of pitting the native intelligence
of women against the native sentimentality of men,
and the other half consists of bringing women into a
reasonable order, that their superiority may not be
too horribly obvious.   To the first division belong
the dramas of courtship, and a good many of those
of marital conflict.   In each case the essential drama
is not a tragedy but a comedy—nay, a farce.   In each
case the conflict is not between imperishable verities
but between mere vanities and pretensions.   This is
the essence of the comic: the unmasking of fraud, its
destruction by worse fraud.   Marriage, as we know
it in Christendom, though its utility is obvious and
its necessity is at least arguable, is just such a series
of frauds.   It begins with the fraud that the impulse
to it is lofty, unearthly and disinterested.   It proceeds to the fraud that both parties are equally eager
for it and equally benefited by it—which actually
happens only when two Mondays come together.
And it rests thereafter upon the fraud that what is
once agreeable (or tolerable) remains agreeable ever
thereafter—that I shall be exactly the same man in
1938 that I am to-day, and that my wife will be the
same woman, and intrigued by the merits of the same
man.   This last assumption is so outrageous that, on
purely evidential and logical grounds, not even the
most sentimental person would support it.   It thus

becomes necessary to reënforce it by attaching to it the concept of honor. That is to say, it is held up, not on the ground that it is actually true, but on the ground that a recognition of its truth is part of the bargain made at the altar, and that a repudiation of this bargain would be dishonorable. Here we have honor, which is based upon a sense of the deepest and most inviolable truth, brought in to support something admittedly not true. Here, in other words, we have a situation in comedy, almost exactly parallel to that in which a colored bishop whoops "Onward, Christian Soldiers!" like a calliope in order to drown out the crowing of the rooster concealed beneath his chasuble.

In all plays of the sort that are regarded as "strong" and "significant" in Greenwich Village, in the finishing schools and by the newspaper critics, connubial infidelity is the chief theme. Smith, having a wife, Mrs. Smith, betrays her love and trust by running off with Miss Rabinowitz, his stenographer. Or Mrs. Brown, detecting her husband, Mr. Brown, in lamentable proceedings with a neighbor, the grass widow Kraus, forgives him and continues to be true to him in consideration of her children, Fred, Pansy and Little Fern. Both situations produce a great deal of eye-rolling and snuffling among the softies aforesaid. Yet neither contains the slightest touch of tragedy, and neither at bottom is even honest. Both, on the contrary, are based upon an assumption that is unsound and ridiculous—the assumption, to wit, that the position of the injured wife is grounded upon the highest idealism—that the injury she suffers is directed at her lofty and impeccable spirit—that it leaves her standing in an heroic attitude. All this, soberly examined, is found to be untrue. The fact is that her moving impulse is simply a desire to cut a good figure before her world—in brief, that plain vanity is what animates her.

This public expectation that she will endure and renounce is itself hollow and sentimental, and so much so that it can seldom stand much strain. If, for example, her heroism goes beyond a certain modest point—if she carries it to the extent of complete abnegation and self-sacrifice—her reward is not that she is thought heroic, but that she is thought weak and foolish. And if, by any chance, the external pressure upon her is removed and she is left to go on with her alleged idealism alone—if, say, her recreant husband dies and some new suitor enters to dispute the theory of her deathless fidelity—then it is regarded as down-right insane for her to continue playing her artificial part.

In frank comedy we see the situation more accurately dealt with and hence more honestly and more instructively. Instead of depicting one party as revolting against the assumption of eternal fidelity melodramatically and the other as facing the revolt heroically and tragically, we have both criticizing it by a good-humored flouting of it—not necessarily by act, but by attitude. This attitude is normal and sensible. It rests upon genuine human traits and tendencies. It is sound, natural and honest. It gives the comedy of the stage a high validity that the bombastic fustian of the stage can never show, all the sophomores to the contrary notwithstanding.

When I speak of infidelity, of course, I do not mean only the gross infidelity of "strong" sex plays and the divorce courts, but that lighter infidelity which relieves and makes bearable the burdens of theoretical fidelity—in brief, the natural reaction of human nature against an artificial and preposterous assumption. The assumption is that a sexual choice, once made, is irrevocable—more, that all desire to revoke it, even transiently, disappears. The fact is that no human choice can ever be of that irrevocable character, and that the very existence of such an assumption is a constant provocation to challenge it and rebel against it.

What we have in marriage actually—or in any other such contract—is a constant war between the impulse to give that rebellion objective reality and a social pressure which puts a premium on submission. The rebel, if he strikes out, at once collides with a solid wall, the bricks of which are made up of the social assumption of his docility, and the mortar of which is the frozen sentimentality of his own lost yesterday—his fatuous assumption that what was once agreeable to him would be always agreeable to him. Here we have the very essence of comedy—a situation almost exactly parallel to that of the pompous old gentleman who kicks a plug hat lying on the sidewalk, and stumps his toe against the cobblestone within.

Under the whole of the conventional assumption reposes an assumption even more foolish, to wit, that sexual choice is regulated by some transcendental process, that a mysterious accuracy gets into it, that it is limited by impenetrable powers, that there is for every man one certain woman. This sentimentality not only underlies the theory of marriage, but is also the chief apology for divorce. Nothing could be more ridiculous. The truth is that marriages in Christendom are determined, not by elective affinities, but by the most trivial accidents, and that the issue of those accidents is relatively unimportant. That is to say, a normal man could be happy with any one of at least two dozen women of his acquaintance, and a man specially fitted to accept the false assumptions of marriage could be happy with almost any presentable woman of his race, class and age. He is married to Marie instead of to Gladys because Marie definitely decided to marry him, whereas Gladys vacillated between him and some other. And Marie decided to marry him instead of some other, not because the impulse was irresistibly stronger, but simply because the thing seemed more feasible.   In such choices, at least among women, there is often not even any self-delusion.   They see the facts clearly, and even if, later on, they are swathed in sentimental trappings, the revelation is not entirely obliterated.

Here we have comedy double distilled—a combat of pretensions, on the one side, perhaps, risen to self-hallucination, but on the other side more or less uneasily conscious and deliberate.   This is the true soul of high farce.   This is something not to snuffle over but to roar at.

XVII. GEORGE JEAN NATHAN

ONE thinks of Gordon Craig, not as a jester, but as a very serious and even solemn fellow. For a dozen years past all the more sober dramatic critics of America have approached him with the utmost politeness, and to the gushing old maids and autointoxicated professors of the Drama League of America he has stood for the last word in theatrical æstheticism. Moreover, a good deal of this veneration has been deserved, for Craig has done excellent work in the theater, and is a man of much force and ingenuity and no little originality. Nevertheless, there must be some flavor of low, barroom wit in him, some echo of Sir Toby Belch and the Captain of Köpenick, for a year or so ago he shook up his admirers with a joke most foul. . Need I say that I refer to the notorious Nathan affair? Imagine the scene: the campus Archers and Walkleys in ponderous conclave, perhaps preparing their monthly cablegram of devotion to Maeterlinck. Arrives now a messenger with dreadful news. Gordon Craig, from his far-off Italian retreat, has issued a bull praising Nathan! Which Nathan? George Jean, of course. What! The *Smart Set* scaramouche, the ribald fellow, the raffish mocker, with his praise of Florenz Ziegfeld, his naughty enthusiasm for pretty legs, his contumacious scoffing at Brieux, Belasco, Augustus Thomas, Mrs. Fiske? Aye; even so. And what has Craig to say of him? . . . In brief, that he is the *only* American dramatic critic worth reading, that he knows far more about the theater than all the honorary pallbearers of criticism rolled together, that he is immeasurably the superior, in learning, in sense, in shrewdness, in candor, in plausibility, in skill at writing, of—

But names do not matter. Craig, in fact, did not bother to rehearse them. He simply made a clean sweep of the board, and then deftly placed the somewhat disconcerted Nathan in the center of the vacant space. It was a sad day for the honest donkeys who, for half a decade, had been laboriously establishing Craig's authority in America, but it was a glad day for Knopf, the publisher. Knopf, at the moment, had just issued Nathan's "The Popular Theater." At once he rushed to a job printer in Eighth avenue, ordered 100,000 copies of the Craig encomium, and flooded the country with them. The result was amusing, and typical of the republic. Nathan's previous books, when praised at all, had been praised faintly and with reservations. The fellow, it appeared, was too spoofish; he lacked the sobriety and

210 PREJUDICES: FIRST SERIES

dignity necessary to a True Critic; he was entertaining
but not to be taken seriously.   But now, with foreign
backing, and particularly English backing, he suddenly began to acquire merit and even a certain vague
solemnity—and "The Popular Theater" was reviewed
more lavishly and more favorably than I have ever
seen any other theater book reviewed, before or since.
The phenomenon, as I say, was typical.   The childish
mass of superstitions passing for civilized opinion in
America was turned inside out over-night by one au-
thoritative foreign voice.   I have myself been a
figure in the same familiar process.   All of my books
up to "The American Language" were, in the main,
hostilely noticed.   "A Book of Prefaces," in particular, was manhandled by the orthodox reviewers.
Then, just before "The American Language" was
issued, the *Mercure de France* printed an article com-
mending "A Book of Prefaces" in high, astounding
terms.   The consequence was that "The American
Language," a far inferior work, was suddenly discovered to be full of merit, and critics of the utmost
respectability, who had ignored all my former books,
printed extremely friendly reviews of it. . . .

But to return to Nathan.   What deceived the
Drama Leaguers and other such imposing popinjays
for so long, causing them to mistake him for a mere
sublimated Alan Dale, was his refusal to take imbecilities seriously, his easy casualness and avoidance

of pedagogics, his frank delight in the theater as a show-shop—above all, his bellicose iconoclasm and devastating wit. What Craig, an intelligent man, discerned underneath was his extraordinary capacity for differentiating between sham and reality, his catholic freedom from formulæ and prejudice, his astonishing acquaintance with the literature of the practical theater, his firm grounding in rational æsthetic theory—above all, his capacity for making the thing he writes of interesting, his uncommon craftsmanship. This craftsmanship had already got him a large audience; he had been for half a dozen years, indeed, one of the most widely read of American dramatic critics. But the traditional delusion that sagacity and dullness are somehow identical had obscured the hard and accurate thinking that made the show. What was so amusing seemed necessarily superficial. It remained for Craig to show that this appearance of superficiality was only an appearance, that the Nathan criticism was well planned and soundly articulated, that at the heart of it there was a sound theory of the theater, and of the literature of the theater no less.

And what was that theory? You will find it nowhere put into a ready formula, but the outlines of it must surely be familiar to any one who has read "Another Book on the Theater," "The Popular Theater" and "Mr. George Jean Nathan Presents."

In brief, it is the doctrine preached with so much ardor by Benedetto Croce and his disciple, Dr. J. E. Spingarn, and by them borrowed from Goethe and Carlyle—the doctrine, to wit, that every work of art is, at bottom, unique, and that it is the business of the critic, not to label it and pigeon-hole it, but to seek for its inner intent and content, and to value it according as that intent is carried out and that content is valid and worth while. This is the precise opposite of the academic critical attitude. The professor is nothing if not a maker of card-indexes; he must classify or be damned. His masterpiece is the dictum that "it is excellent, but it is not a play." Nathan has a far more intelligent and hospitable eye. His criterion, elastic and undefined, is inimical only to the hollow, the meretricious, the fraudulent. It bars out the play of flabby and artificial sentiment. It bars out the cheap melodrama, however gaudily set forth. It bars out the moony mush of the bad imitators of Ibsen and Maeterlinck. It bars out all mere clap-trap and sensation-monging. But it lets in every play, however conceived or designed, that contains an intelligible idea well worked out. It lets in every play by a dramatist who is ingenious, and original, and genuinely amusing. And it lets in every other sort of theatrical spectacle that has an honest aim, and achieves that aim passably, and is presented frankly for what it is.

Bear this theory in mind, and you have a clear explanation of Nathan's actual performances—first, his merciless lampooning of the trade-goods of Broadway and the pifflings of the Drama League geniuses, and secondly, his ardent championing of such widely diverse men as Avery Hopwood, Florenz Ziegfeld, Ludwig Thoma, Lord Dunsany, Sasha Guitry, Lothar Schmidt, Ferenz Molnar, Roberto Bracco and Gerhart Hauptmann, all of whom have one thing in common: they are intelligent and full of ideas and know their trade. In Europe, of course, there are many more such men than in America, and some of the least of them are almost as good as our best. That is why Nathan is forever announcing them and advocating the presentation of their works—not because he favors foreignness for its own sake, but because it is so often accompanied by sound achievement and by stimulating example to our own artists. And that is why, when he tackles the maudlin flubdub of the Broadway dons, he does it with the weapons of comedy, and even of farce. Does an Augustus Thomas rise up with his corn-doctor magic and Sunday-school platitudes, proving heavily that love is mightier than the sword, that a pure heart will baffle the electric chair, that the eye is quicker than the hand? Then Nathan proceeds against him with a slapstick, and makes excellent practice upon his pantaloons. Does a Belasco, thumb on forelock, posture before the yeomanry as a Great Artist, the evidence being a large chromo of a Childs' restaurant, and a studio like a Madison avenue antique-shop? Then Nathan flings a laugh at him and puts him in his place. And does some fat rhinoceros of an actress, unearthing a smutty play by a corn-fed Racine, loose its banal obscenities upon the vulgar in the name of Sex Hygiene, presuming thus to teach a Great Lesson, and break the Conspiracy of Silence, and carry on the Noble Work of Brieux and company, and so save impatient flappers from the Moloch's Sacrifice of the Altar—does such a bumptious and preposterous baggage fill the newspapers with her pishposh and the largest theater in Manhattan with eager dunderheads? Then the ribald Jean has at her with a flour-sack filled with the pollen of the *Ambrosia artemisiaefolia*, driving her from the scene to the tune of her own unearthly sneezing.

Necessarily, he has to lay on with frequency. For one honest play, honestly produced and honestly played, Broadway sees two dozen that are simply so much green-goods. To devote serious exposition to the badness of such stuff would be to descend to the donkeyish futility of William Winter. Sometimes, indeed, even ridicule is not enough; there must be a briefer and more dramatic display of the essential banality. Well, then, why not recreate it in the manner of Croce—but touching up a line here, a color

there? The result is burlesque, but burlesque that is
the most searching and illuminating sort of criticism.
Who will forget Nathan's demonstration that a platitudinous play by Thomas would be better if played
backward? A superb bravura piece, enormously
beyond the talents of any other American writer on
the theater, it smashed the Thomas legend with one
stroke. In the little volume called "Bottoms Up"
you will find many other such annihilating waggeries.
Nathan does not denounce melodrama with a black
cap upon his head, painfully demonstrating its inferiority to the drama of Ibsen, Scribe and Euripides;
he simply sits down and writes a little melodrama so
extravagantly ludicrous that the whole genus col-
lapses. And he does not prove in four columns of a
Sunday paper that French plays done into American
are spoiled; he simply shows the spoiling in six lines.

This method, of course, makes for broken heads;
it outrages the feelings of tender theatrical mountebanks; it provokes reprisals more or less furtive and
behind the door. The theater in America, as in most
other countries, is operated chiefly by bounders. Men
so constantly associated with actors tend to take on
the qualities of the actor—his idiotic vanity, his herculean stupidity, his chronic underrating of his betters. The miasma spreads to dramatists and dramatic
critics; the former drift into charlatanery and the
latter into a cowardly and disgusting dishonesty.

Amid such scenes a man of positive ideas, of civilized tastes and of unshakable integrity is a stranger, and he must face all the hostility that the lower orders of men display to strangers.   There is, so far as I know, no tripe-seller in Broadway who has not tried, at one time or another, to dispose of Nathan by *attentat*.   He has been exposed to all the measures ordinarily effective against rebellious reviewers, and, resisting them, he has been treated to special treatment with infernal machines of novel and startling design.   No writer for the theater has been harder beset, and none has been less incommoded by the onslaught.   What is more, he has never made the slightest effort to capitalize this drum-fire—the invariable device of lesser men.   So far as I am aware, and I have been in close association with him for ten years, it has had not the slightest effect upon him whatsoever.   A thoroughgoing skeptic, with no trace in him of the messianic delusion, he has avoided timorousness on the one hand and indignation on the other.   No man could be less a public martyr of the Metcalfe type; it would probably amuse him vastly to hear it argued that his unbreakable independence (and often somewhat high and mighty sniffishness) has been of any public usefulness.   I sometimes wonder what keeps such a man in the theater, breathing bad air nightly, gaping at prancing imbeciles, sitting cheek by jowl with cads.   Perhaps there is, at bottom, a secret romanticism—a lingering residuum of a boyish delight in pasteboard and spangles, gaudy colors and soothing sounds, preposterous heroes and appetizing wenches. But more likely it is a sense of humor—the zest of a man to whom life is a spectacle that never grows dull—a show infinitely surprising, amusing, buffoonish, vulgar, obscene. The theater, when all is said and done, is not life in miniature, but life enormously magnified, life hideously exaggerated. Its emotions are ten times as powerful as those of reality, its ideas are twenty times as idiotic as those of real men, its lights and colors and sounds are forty times as blinding and deafening as those of nature, its people are grotesque burlesques of every one we know. Here is diversion for a cynic. And here, it may be, is the explanation of Nathan's fidelity.

Whatever the cause of his enchantment, it seems to be lasting. To a man so fertile in ideas and so facile in putting them into words there is a constant temptation to make experiments, to plunge into strange waters, to seek self-expression in ever-widening circles. And yet, at the brink of forty years, Nathan remains faithful to the theater; of his half dozen books, only one does not deal with it, and that one is a very small one. In four or five years he has scarcely written of aught else. I doubt that anything properly describable as enthusiasm is at the bottom of this assiduity; perhaps the right word is curiosity. He is interested mainly, not in the staple fare of the playhouse, but in what might be called its fancy goods —in its endless stream of new men, its restless innovations, the radical overhauling that it has been undergoing in our time. I do not recall, in any of his books or articles, a single paragraph appraising the classics of the stage, or more than a brief note or two on their interpretation. His attention is always turned in a quite opposite direction. He is intensely interested in novelty of whatever sort, if it be only free from sham. Such experimentalists as Max Reinhardt, George Bernard Shaw, Sasha Guitry and the daring nobodies of the Grand Guignol, such divergent originals as Dunsany, Ziegfeld, George M. Cohan and Schnitzler, have enlisted his eager partisanship. He saw something new to our theater in the farces of Hopwood before any one else saw it; he was quick to welcome the novel points of view of Eleanor Gates and Clare Kummer; he at once rescued what was sound in the Little Theatre movement from what was mere attitudinizing and pseudo-intellectuality. In the view of Broadway, an exigent and even malignant fellow, wielding a pen dipped in *aqua fortis*, he is actually amiable to the last degree, and constantly announces pearls in the fodder of the swine. Is the new play in Forty-second Street a serious work of art, as the press-agents and the newspaper reviewers say?

Then so are your grandmother's false teeth! Is
Maeterlinck a Great Thinker? Then so is Dr. Frank
Crane! Is Belasco a profound artist? Then so is
the man who designs the ceilings of hotel dining
rooms! But let us not weep too soon. In the play
around the corner there is a clever scene. Next door,
amid sickening dullness, there are two buffoons who
could be worse: one clouts the other with a *Blutwurst*
filled with mayonnaise. And a block away there is a
girl in the second row with a very charming twist of
the *vastus medialis*. Let us sniff the roses and forget
the thorns!

What this attitude chiefly wars with, even above
cheapness, meretriciousness and banality, is the
fatuous effort to turn the theater, a place of amuse-
ment, into a sort of outhouse to the academic grove—
the Maeterlinck-Brieux-Barker complex. No critic
in America, and none in England save perhaps
Walkley, has combated this movement more vigorously than Nathan. He is under no illusion as to the
functions and limitations of the stage. He knows,
with Victor Hugo, that the best it can do, in the
domain of ideas, is to "turn thoughts into food for the
crowd," and he knows that only the simplest and
shakiest ideas may undergo that transformation.
Coming upon the scene at the height of the Ibsen
mania of half a generation ago, he ranged himself
against its windy pretenses from the start. He saw

at once the high merit of Ibsen as a dramatic craftsman and welcomed him as a reformer of dramatic
technique, but he also saw how platitudinous was the
ideational content of his plays and announced the
fact in terms highly offensive to the Ibsenites. . . .
But the Ibsenites have vanished and Nathan remains.
He has survived, too, the Brieux hubbub. He has
lived to preach the funeral sermon of the Belasco
legend. He has himself sworded Maeterlinck and
Granville Barker. He has done frightful execution
upon many a poor mime. And meanwhile, breasting
the murky tide of professorial buncombe, of solemn
pontificating, of Richard-Burtonism, Clayton-Hamil-
tonism and other such decaying forms of William-
Winterism, he has rescued dramatic criticism among
us from its exile with theology, embalming and obstetrics, and given it a place among what Nietzsche
called the gay sciences, along with war, fiddle-playing
and laparotomy. He has made it amusing, stimulating, challenging, even, at times, a bit startling. And
to the business, artfully concealed, he has brought a
sound and thorough acquaintance with the heavy work
of the pioneers, Lessing, Schlegel, Hazlitt, Lewes *et al*
—and an even wider acquaintance, lavishly displayed, with every nook and corner of the current
theatrical scene across the water. And to discharge
this extraordinarily copious mass of information he

has hauled and battered the English language into new and often astounding forms, and when English has failed he has helped it out with French, German, Italian, American, Swedish, Russian, Turkish, Latin, Sanskrit and Old Church Slavic, and with algebraic symbols, chemical formulæ, musical notation and the signs of the Zodiac. . . .

This manner, of course, is not without its perils. A man so inordinately articulate is bound to succumb, now and then, to the seductions of mere virtuosity. The average writer, and particularly the average critic of the drama, does well if he gets a single new and racy phrase into an essay; Nathan does well if he dilutes his inventions with enough commonplaces to enable the average reader to understand his discourse at all. He carries the avoidance of the *cliché* to the length of an *idée fixe*. It would be difficult, in all his books, to find a dozen of the usual rubber stamps of criticism; I daresay it would kill him, or, at all events, bring him down with cholera morbus, to discover that he had called a play "convincing" or found "authority" in the snorting of an English actor-manager. At best, this incessant flight from the obvious makes for a piquant and arresting style, a procession of fantastic and often highly pungent neologisms—in brief, for Nathanism. At worst, it becomes artificiality, pedantry, obscurity. I cite an example from an essay on Eleanor Gates' "The Poor Little Rich Girl," prefaced to the printed play:

> As against the not unhollow symbolic strut and gasconade of such over-pæaned pieces as, let us for example say, "The Blue Bird" of Maeterlinck, so simple and unaffected a bit of stage writing as this—of school dramatic intrinsically the same—cajoles the more honest heart and satisfies more plausibly and fully those of us whose thumbs are ever being pulled professionally for a native stage less smeared with the snobberies of empty, albeit high-sounding, nomenclatures from overseas.

Fancy that, Hedda!—and in praise of a "simple and unaffected bit of stage writing"! I denounced it at the time, *circa* 1916, and perhaps with some effect. At all events, I seem to notice a gradual disentanglement of the parts of speech. The old florid invention is still there; one encounters startling coinages in even the most casual of reviews; the thing still flashes and glitters; the tune is yet upon the E string. But underneath I hear a more sober rhythm than of old. The fellow, in fact, takes on a sedater habit, both in style and in point of view. Without abandoning anything essential, without making the slightest concession to the orthodox opinion that he so magnificently disdains, he yet begins to yield to the middle years. The mere shocking of the stupid is no longer as charming as it used to be. What he now offers is rather more *gemütlich;* sometimes it even verges upon

GEORGE JEAN NATHAN   223

the instructive. . . . But I doubt that Nathan will ever become a professor, even if he enjoys the hideously prolonged senility of a William Winter. He will be full of surprises to the end. With his last gasp he will make a phrase to flabbergast a dolt.

XVIII. PORTRAIT OF AN
IMMORTAL SOUL

ONE day in Spring, six or eight years ago, I
received a letter from a man somewhere
beyond the Wabash announcing that he had
lately completed a very powerful novel and hinting
that my critical judgment upon it would give him
great comfort. Such notifications, at that time,
reached me far too often to be agreeable, and so I
sent him a form-response telling him that I was ill
with pleurisy, had just been forbidden by my oculist
to use my eyes, and was about to become a father.
The aim of this form-response was to shunt all that
sort of trade off to other reviewers, but for once it
failed. That is to say, the unknown kept on writing
to me, and finally offered to pay me an honorarium
for my labor. This offer was so unusual that it quite
demoralized me, and before I could recover I had received, cashed and dissipated a modest check, and
was confronted by an accusing manuscript, perhaps
four inches thick, but growing thicker every time I
glanced at it.

One night, tortured by conscience and by the inquiries and reminders arriving from the author by

every post, I took up the sheets and settled down for
a depressing hour or two of it. . . . No, I did *not*
read all night. No, it was *not* a masterpiece. No, it
has *not* made the far-off stranger famous. Let me
tell the story quite honestly. I am, in fact, far too
rapid a reader to waste a whole night on a novel; I
had got through this one by midnight and was sound
asleep at my usual time. And it was by no means a
masterpiece; on the contrary, it was inchoate, clumsy,
and, in part, artificial, insincere and preposterous.
And to this day the author remains obscure. . . .
But underneath all the amateurish writing, the striv-
ing for effects that failed to come off, the absurd literary self-consciousness, the recurrent falsity and banality—underneath all these stigmata of a neophyte's
book there was yet a capital story, unusual in content, naïve in manner and enormously engrossing.
What is more, the faults that it showed in execution
were, most of them, not ineradicable. On page after
page, as I read on, I saw chances to improve it—to
get rid of its intermittent bathos, to hasten its action,
to eliminate its spells of fine writing, to purge it of
its imitations of all the bad novels ever written—in
brief, to tighten it, organize it, and, as the painters
say, tease it up.

The result was that I spent the next morning writing the author a long letter of advice. It went to him
with the manuscript, and for weeks I heard nothing

from him. Then the manuscript returned, and I
read it again. This time I had a genuine surprise.
Not only had the unknown followed my suggestions
with much intelligence; in addition, once set up on the
right track, he had devised a great many excellent
improvements of his own. In its new form, in fact,
the thing was a very competent and even dexterous
piece of writing, and after re-reading it from the
first word to the last with even keener interest than
before, I sent it to Mitchell Kennerley, then an active
publisher, and asked him to look through it. Kennerley made an offer for it at once, and eight or
nine months later it was published with his imprint.
The author chose to conceal himself behind the *nom
de plume* of Robert Steele; I myself gave the book
the title of "One Man." It came from the press—
and straightway died the death. The only favorable
review it received was mine in the *Smart Set*. No
other reviewer paid any heed to it. No one gabbled
about it. No one, so far as I could make out, even
read it. The sale was small from the start, and
quickly stopped altogether. . . . To this day the fact
fills me with wonder. To this day I marvel that so
dramatic, so penetrating and so curiously moving a
story should have failed so overwhelmingly. . . .

For I have never been able to convince myself that
I was wrong about it. On the contrary, I am more
certain than ever, re-reading it after half a dozen

years, that I was right—that it was and is one of the most honest and absorbing human documents ever printed in America. I have called it, following the author, a novel. It is, in fact, nothing of the sort; it is autobiography. More, it is autobiography unadorned and shameless, autobiography almost unbelievably cruel and betraying, autobiography that is as devoid of artistic sophistication as an operation for gall-stones. This so-called Steele is simply too stupid, too ingenuous, too moral to lie. He is the very reverse of an artist; he is a born and incurable Puritan—and in his alleged novel he draws the most faithful and merciless picture of an American Puritan that has ever got upon paper. There is never the slightest effort at amelioration; he never evades the ghastly horror of it; he never tries to palm off himself as a good fellow, a hero. Instead, he simply takes his stand in the center of the platform, where all the spotlights meet, and there calmly strips off his raiment of reticence—first his Sunday plug-hat, then his long-tailed coat, then his boiled shirt, then his shoes and socks, and finally his very B. V. D.'s. The closing scene shows the authentic *Mensch-an-sich*, the eternal blue-nose in the nude, with every wart and pimple glittering and every warped bone and flabby muscle telling its abhorrent tale. There stands the Puritan stripped of every artifice and concealment, like Thackeray's Louis XIV.

Searching my memory, I can drag up no recollection of another such self-opener of secret chambers and skeletonic closets. Set beside this pious babbler, the late Giovanni Jacopo Casanova de Seingalt shrinks to the puny proportions of a mere barroom boaster, a smoking-car Don Juan, an Eighteenth Century stock company leading man or whiskey drummer. So, too, Benvenuto Cellini: a fellow vastly entertaining, true enough, but after all, not so much a psychological historian as a liar, a yellow journalist. One always feels, in reading Benvenuto, that the man who is telling the story is quite distinct from the man about whom it is being told. The fellow, indeed, was too noble an artist to do a mere portrait with fidelity; he could not resist the temptation to repair a cauliflower ear here, to paint out a tell-tale scar there, to shine up the eyes a bit, to straighten the legs down below. But this Steele—or whatever his name may be—never steps out of himself. He is never describing the gaudy one he would *like* to be, but always the commonplace, the weak, the emotional, the ignorant, the third-rate Christian male that he actually is. He deplores himself, he distrusts himself, he plainly wishes heartily that he was not himself, but he never makes the slightest attempt to disguise and bedizen himself. Such as he is, cheap, mawkish, unæsthetic, conscience-stricken, he depicts himself with fierce and unrelenting honesty.

Superficially, the man that he sets before us seems to be a felonious fellow, for he confesses frankly to a long series of youthful larcenies, to a somewhat banal adventure in forgery (leading to a term in jail), to sundry petty deceits and breaches of trust, and to an almost endless chain of exploits in amour, most of them sordid and unrelieved by anything approaching romance. But the inner truth about him, of course, is that he is really a moralist of the moralists—that his one fundamental and all-embracing virtue is what he himself regards as his viciousness —that he is never genuinely human and likable save in those moments which lead swiftly to his most florid self-accusing. In brief, the history is that of a moral young man, the child of God-fearing parents, and its moral, if it has one, is that a strictly moral upbringing injects poisons into the system that even the most steadfast morality cannot resist. It is, in a way, the old story of the preacher's son turned sot and cutthroat.

Here we see an apparently sound and normal youngster converted into a sneak and rogue by the intolerable pressure of his father's abominable Puritanism. And once a rogue, we see him make himself into a scoundrel by the very force of his horror of his roguery. Every step downward is helped from above. It is not until he resigns himself frankly to the fact of his incurable degradation, and so ceases to struggle against it, that he ever steps out of it.

The external facts of the chronicle are simple enough. The son of a school teacher turned petty lawyer and politician, the hero is brought up under such barbaric rigors that he has already become a fluent and ingenious liar, in sheer self-protection, at the age of five or six. From lying he proceeds quite naturally to stealing: he lifts a few dollars from a neighbor, and then rifles a tin bank, and then takes to filching all sorts of small articles from the store-keepers of the vicinage. His harsh, stupid, Christian father, getting wind of these peccadilloes, has at him in the manner of a mad bull, beating him, screaming at him, half killing him. The boy, for all the indecent cruelty of it, is convinced of the justice of it. He sees himself as one lost; he accepts the fact that he is a disgrace to his family; in the end, he embraces the parental theory that there is something strange and sinister in his soul, that he couldn't be good if he tried. Finally, filled with some vague notion of taking his abhorrent self out of sight, he runs away from home. Brought back in the character of a felon, he runs away again. Soon he is a felon in fact. That is to say, he forges his father's name to a sheaf of checks, and his father allows him to go to prison.

This prison term gives the youngster a chance to

think things out for himself, without the constant intrusion of his father's Presbyterian notions of right or wrong. The result is a measurably saner philosophy than that he absorbed at home, but there is still enough left of the old moral obsession to cripple him in all his thinking, and especially in his thinking about himself. His attitude toward women, for example, is constantly conditioned by puritanical misgivings and superstitions. He can never view them innocently, joyously, unmorally, as a young fellow of twenty or twenty-one should, but is always oppressed by Sunday-schoolish notions of his duty to them, and to society in general. On the one hand, he is appalled by his ready yielding to those hussies who have at him unofficially, and on the other hand he is filled with the idea that it would be immoral for him, an ex-convict, to go to the altar with a virgin. The result of these doubts is that he gives a good deal more earnest thought to the woman question than is good for him. The second result is that he proves an easy victim to the discarded mistress of his employer. This worthy working girl craftily snares him and marries him—and then breaks down on their wedding night, unwomaned, so to speak, by the pathetic innocence of the ass, and confesses to a choice roll of her past doings, ending with the news that she is suffering from what the vice crusaders mellifluously denominate a "social disease."

Naturally enough, the blow almost kills the poor boy—he is still, in fact, scarcely out of his nonage—and the problems that grow out of the confession engage him for the better part of the next two years. Always he approaches them and wrestles with them morally; always his search is for the way that the copy-book maxims approve, not for the way that self-preservation demands. Even when a brilliant chance for revenge presents itself, and he is forced to embrace it by the sheer magnetic pull of it, he does so hesitatingly, doubtingly, ashamedly. His whole attitude to this affair, indeed, is that of an Early Christian Father. He hates himself for gathering rosebuds while he may; he hates the woman with a double hatred for strewing them so temptingly in his path. And in the end, like the moral and upright fellow that he is, he sells out the temptress for cash in hand, and salves his conscience by handing over the money to an orphan asylum. This after prayers for divine guidance. A fact! Don't miss the story of it in the book. You will go far before you get another such illuminating glimpse into a pure and righteous mind.

So in episode after episode. One observes a constant oscillation between a pharisaical piety and a hoggish carnality. The praying brother of yesterday is the night-hack roisterer of to-day; the roisterer of to-day is the snuffling penitent and pledge-taker of to-morrow. Finally, he is pulled both ways at once

and suffers the greatest of all his tortures. Again,
of course, a woman is at the center of it—this time
a stenographer. He has no delusions about her virtue—she admits herself, in fact, that it is extinct—
but all the same he falls head over heels in love with
her, and is filled with an inordinate yearning to marry
her and settle down with her. Why not, indeed?
She is pretty and a nice girl; she seems to reciprocate
his affection; she is naturally eager for the obliterat-
ing gold band; she will undoubtedly make him an
excellent wife. But he has forgotten his conscience
—and it rises up in revenge and floors him. What!
Marry a girl with such a Past! Take a fancy woman
to his bosom! Jealousy quickly comes to the aid of
conscience. Will he be able to forget? Contemplat-
ing the damsel in the years to come, at breakfast, at
dinner, across the domestic hearth, in the cold, blue
dawn, will he ever rid his mind of those abhorrent
images, those phantasms of men?

Here, at the very end, we come to the most engrossing chapter in this extraordinary book. The
duelist of sex, thrust through the gizzard at last, goes
off to a lonely hunting camp to wrestle with his intolerable problem. He describes his vacillations
faithfully, elaborately, cruelly. On the one side he
sets his honest yearning, his desire to have done with
light loves, the girl herself. On the other hand he
ranges his moral qualms, his sneaking distrusts, the

sinister shadows of those nameless ones, his morgan-
atic brothers-in-law. The struggle within his soul is
gigantic. He suffers as Prometheus suffered on the
rock; his very vitals are devoured; he emerges battered and exhausted. He decides, in the end, that
he will marry the girl. She has wasted the shining
dowry of her sex; she comes to him spotted and at
second-hand; snickers will appear in the polyphony
of the wedding music—but he will marry her nevertheless. It will be a marriage unblessed by Holy
Writ; it will be a flying in the face of Moses; luck
and the archangels will be against it—but he will
marry her all the same, Moses or no Moses. And so,
with his face made bright by his first genuine revolt
against the archaic, barbaric morality that has
dragged him down, and his heart pulsing to his first
display of authentic, unpolluted charity, generosity
and nobility, he takes his departure from us. May
the fates favor him with their mercy! May the Lord
God strain a point to lift him out of his purgatory
at last! He has suffered all the agonies of belief.
He has done abominable penance for the Westminster
Catechism, and for the moral order of the world,
and for all the despairing misery of back-street, black
bombazine, Little Bethel goodness. He is Puritanism
incarnate, and Puritanism become intolerable. . . .

I daresay any second-hand bookseller will be able
to find a copy of the book for you: "One Man," by

Robert Steele. There is some raciness in the detail of it. Perhaps, despite its public failure, it enjoys a measure of *pizzicato* esteem behind the door. The author, having achieved its colossal self-revelation, became intrigued by the notion that he was a literary man of sorts, and informed me that he was undertaking the story of the girl last-named—the spotted ex-virgin. But he apparently never finished it. No doubt he discovered, before he had gone very far, that the tale was intrinsically beyond him—that his fingers all turned into thumbs when he got beyond his own personal history. Such a writer, once he has told the one big story, is done for.

XIX. JACK LONDON

THE quasi-science of genealogy, as it is practiced in the United States, is directed almost exclusively toward establishing aristocratic descents for nobodies. That is to say, it records and glorifies decay. Its typical masterpiece is the discovery that the wife of some obscure county judge is the grandchild, infinitely removed, of Mary Queen of Scots, or that the blood of Geoffrey of Monmouth flows in the veins of a Philadelphia stockbroker. How much more profitably its professors might be employed in tracing the lineage of truly salient and distinguished men! For example, the late Jack London. Where did he get his hot artistic passion, his delicate feeling for form and color, his extraordinary skill with words? The man, in truth, was an instinctive artist of a high order, and if ignorance often corrupted his art, it only made the fact of his inborn mastery the more remarkable. No other popular writer of his time did any better writing than you will find in "The Call of the Wild," or in parts of "John Barleycorn," or in such short stories as "The Sea Farmer" and "Samuel." Here, indeed, are all the elements of sound fiction: clear thinking, a sense of character, the dramatic instinct, and, above all, the adept putting together of words—words charming and slyly significant, words arranged, in a French phrase, for the respiration and the ear. You will never convince me that this æsthetic sensitiveness, so rare, so precious, so distinctively aristocratic, burst into abiogenetic flower on a San Francisco sand-lot. There must have been some intrusion of an alien and superior strain, some *pianissimo* fillup from above; there was obviously a great deal more to the thing than a routine hatching in low life. Perhaps the explanation is to be sought in a Jewish smear. Jews were not few in the California of a generation ago, and one of them, at least, attained to a certain high, if transient, fame with the pen. Moreover, the name, London, has a Jewish smack; the Jews like to call themselves after great cities. I have, indeed, heard this possibility of an Old Testament descent put into an actual rumor. Stranger genealogies are not unknown in seaports. . . .

But London the artist did not live *a cappella*. There was also London the amateur Great Thinker, and the second often hamstrung the first. That great thinking of his, of course, took color from the sordid misery of his early life; it was, in the main, a jejune Socialism, wholly uncriticised by humor. Some of his propagandist and expository books are almost

unbelievably nonsensical, and whenever he allowed
any of his so-called ideas to sneak into an imaginative
work the intrusion promptly spoiled it. Socialism,
in truth, is quite incompatible with art; its cook-tent
materialism is fundamentally at war with the first
principle of the æsthetic gospel, which is that one
daffodil is worth ten shares of Bethlehem Steel. It
is not by accident that there has never been a book
on Socialism which was also a work of art. Papa
Marx's "Das Kapital" at once comes to mind. It
is as wholly devoid of graces as "The Origin of Species" or "Science and Health"; one simply cannot
conceive a reasonable man reading it without aver-
sion; it is as revolting as a barrel organ. London,
preaching Socialism, or quasi-Socialism, or whatever
it was that he preached, took over this offensive dullness. The materialistic conception of history was
too heavy a load for him to carry. When he would
create beautiful books he had to throw it overboard
as Wagner threw overboard democracy, the superman and free thought. A sort of temporary Christian created "Parsifal." A sort of temporary aris-
tocrat created "The Call of the Wild."

Also in another way London's early absorption of
social and economic nostrums damaged him as an
artist. It led him into a socialistic exaltation of
mere money; it put a touch of avarice into him.
Hence his too deadly industry, his relentless thou-

sand words a day, his steady emission of half-done books. The prophet of freedom, he yet sold himself into slavery to the publishers, and paid off with his soul for his ranch, his horses, his trappings of a wealthy cheese-monger. His volumes rolled out almost as fast as those of E. Phillips Oppenheim; he simply could not make them perfect at such a gait. There are books on his list—for example, "The Scarlet Plague" and "The Little Lady of the Big House" —that are little more than garrulous notes for books.

But even in the worst of them one comes upon sudden splashes of brilliant color, stray proofs of the adept penman, half-wistful reminders that London, at bottom, was no fraud. He left enough, I am convinced, to keep him in mind. There was in him a vast delicacy of perception, a high feeling, a sensitiveness to beauty. And there was in him, too, under all his blatancies, a poignant sense of the infinite romance and mystery of human life.

XX. AMONG THE AVATARS

IT may be, as they say, that we Americanos lie in
the gutter of civilization, but all the while our
eyes steal cautious glances at the stars. In the
midst of the prevailing materialism—the thin incense
of mysticism. As a relief from money drives, politics and the struggle for existence—Rosicrucianism,
the Knights of Pythias, passwords, grips, secret work,
the 33rd degree. In flight from Peruna, Mandrake
Pills and Fletcherism—Christian Science, the
Emmanuel Movement, the New Thought. The tendency already has its poets: Edwin Markham and
Ella Wheeler Wilcox. It has acquired its romancer:
Will Levington Comfort. . . .

This Comfort wields an easy pen. He has done,
indeed, some capital melodramas, and when his ardor
heats him up he grows downright eloquent. But of
late the whole force of his æsthetic engines has been
thrown into propaganda, by the Bhagavad-Gitā out
of Victorian sentimentalism. The nature of this
propaganda is quickly discerned. What Comfort
preaches is a sort of mellowed mariolatry, a humorless exaltation of woman, a flashy effort to turn

the inter-attraction of the sexes, ordinarily a mere
cause of scandal, into something transcendental and
highly portentous. Woman, it appears, is the be-
yond-man, the trans-mammal, the nascent angel; she
is the Upward Path, the Way to Consecration, the
door to the Third Lustrous Dimension; all the myster-
ies of the cosmos are concentrated in Mystic Motherhood, whatever that may be. I capitalize in the
Comfortian (and New Thought) manner. On one
page of "Fate Knocks at the Door" I find Voices,
Pits of Trade, Woman, the Great Light, the Big
Deep and the Twentieth Century Lie. On another
are the Rising Road of Man, the Transcendental Soul
Essence, the Way Uphill, the Sempiternal Mother.
Thus Andrew Bedient, the spouting hero of the tale:

I believe in the natural greatness of Woman; that through
the spirit of Woman are born sons of strength; that only
through the potential greatness of Woman comes the mili-
tant greatness of man.

I believe Mothering is the loveliest of the Arts; that
great mothers are handmaidens of the Spirit, to whom are
intrusted God's avatars; that no prophet is greater than
his mother.

I believe when humanity arises to Spiritual evolution
(as it once evolved through Flesh, and is now evolving
through Mind) Woman will assume the ethical guiding
of the race.

I believe that the Holy Spirit of the Trinity is Mystic
Motherhood, and the source of the divine principle is
Woman; that the prophets are the union of this divine

principle and the higher manhood; that they are beyond the attractions of women of flesh, because unto their manhood has been added Mystic Motherhood. . . .

I believe that the way to Godhood is the Rising Road of Man.

I believe that, as the human mother brings a child to her husband, the father—so Mystic Motherhood, the Holy Spirit, is bringing the world to God, the Father.

The capitals are Andrew's—or Comfort's. I merely transcribe and perspire. This Andrew, it appears, is a sea cook who has been mellowed and transfigured by exhaustive study of the Bhagavad Gītā, one of the sacred nonsense books of the Hindus. He doesn't know who his father was, and he remembers his mother only as one dying in a strange city. When she finally passed away he took to the high seas and mastered marine cookery. Thus for many years, up and down the world. Then he went ashore at Manila and became chef to an army packtrain. Then he proceeded to China, to Japan. Then to India, where he entered the forestry service and plodded the Himalayan heights, always with the Bhagavad Gītā under his arm. At some time or other, during his years of culinary seafaring, he saved the life of a Yankee ship captain, and that captain, later dying, left him untold millions in South America. But it is long after all this is past that we have chiefly to do with him. He is now a young Monte Cristo at large in New York, a Monte Cristo worshiped and gurgled over by a crowd of mushy old maids, a hero of Uneeda-biscuit parties in God-forsaken studios, the madness and despair of senescent virgins.

But it is not Andrew's wealth that inflames these old girls, nor even his manly beauty, but rather his revolutionary and astounding sapience, his great gift for solemn and incomprehensible utterance, his skill as a metaphysician. They hang upon his every word. His rhetoric makes their heads swim. Once he gets fully under way, they almost swoon. . . . And what girls they are! Alas, what pathetic neck-stretching toward tinsel stars! What eager hearing of the soulful, gassy stuff! One of them has red hair and "wine dark eyes, now cryptic black, now suffused with red glows like the night sky above a prairie fire." Another is "tall and lovely in a tragic, flower-like way" and performs upon the violoncello. A third is "a tanned woman rather variously weathered," who writes stupefying epigrams about Whitman and Nietzsche—making the latter's name Nietschze, of course! A fourth is "the Gray One"—O mystic appellation! A fifth—but enough! You get the picture. You can imagine how Andrew's sagacity staggers these poor dears. You can see them fighting for him, each against all, with sharp, psychical excaliburs.

Arm in arm with all this exaltation of Woman, of

course, goes a great suspicion of mere woman. The combination is as old as Christian mysticism, and Havelock Ellis has discussed its origin and nature at great length. On the one hand is the *Übermensch;* on the other hand is the temptress, the Lorelei. The Madonna and Mother Eve, the celestial virgins and the succubi! The hero of "Fate Knocks at the Door," for all his flaming words, still distrusts his goddess. His colleague of "Down Among Men" is poisoned by the same suspicions. Woman has led him up to grace, she has shown him the Upward Path, she has illuminated him with her Mystic Motherhood —but the moment she lets go his hand he takes to his heels. What is worse, he sends a friend to her (I forget her name, and his) to explain in detail how unfavorably any further communion with her would corrupt his high mission, *i. e.,* to save the downtrodden by writing plays that fail and books that not even Americans will read. An intellectual milk-toast! A mixture of Dr. Frank Crane and Mother Tingley, of Edward Bok and the Archangel Eddy! . . .

So far, not much of this ineffable stuff has got among the best-sellers, but I believe that it is on its way. Despite materialism and pragmatism, mysticism is steadily growing in fashion. I hear of paunchy Freemasons holding sacramental meetings on Maundy Thursday, of Senators in Congress railing against *materia medica,* of Presidents invoking

divine intercession at Cabinet meetings. The New
Thoughters march on; they have at least a dozen
prosperous magazines, and one of them has a circulation comparable to that of any 20-cent repository of
lingerie fiction. Such things as Karma, the Ineffable Essence and the Zeitgeist become familiar
fauna, chained up in the cage of every woman's club.
Thousands of American women know far more about
the Subconscious than they know about plain sewing.
The pungency of myrrh and frankincense is mingled
with *odeur de femme*. Physiology is formally repealed and repudiated; its laws are all lies. No
doubt the fleshly best-seller of the last decade, with
its blushing amorousness, its flashes of underwear, its
obstetrics between chapters, will give place to a more
delicate piece of trade-goods to-morrow. In this
New Thought novel the hero and heroine will seek
each other out, not to spoon obscenely behind the
door, but for the purpose of uplifting the race. Kissing is already unsanitary; in a few years it may be
downright sacrilegious, a crime against some obscure
avatar or other, a business libidinous and accursed.

XXI. THREE AMERICAN IMMORTALS

1

Aristotelean Obsequies

I TAKE the following from the Boston *Herald* of May 1, 1882:

A beautiful floral book stood at the left of the pulpit, being spread out on a stand. . . . Its last page was composed of white carnations, white daisies and light-colored immortelles. On the leaf was displayed, in neat letters of purple immortelles, the word "Finis." This device was about two feet square, and its border was composed of different colored tea-roses. The other portion of the book was composed of dark and light-colored flowers. . . . The front of the large pulpit was covered with a mass of white pine boughs laid on loosely. In the center of this mass of boughs appeared a large harp composed of yellow jonquils. . . . Above this harp was a handsome bouquet of dark pansies. On each side appeared large clusters of calla lilies.

Well, what have we here? The funeral of a Grand Exalted Pishposh of the Odd Fellows, of an East Side Tammany leader, of an aged and much respected brothel-keeper? Nay. What we have here is the funeral of Ralph Waldo Emerson. It was thus that New England lavished the loveliest fruits of the Puritan æsthetic upon the bier of her greatest son. It was thus that Puritan *Kultur* mourned a philosopher.

2

Edgar Allan Poe

The myth that there is a monument to Edgar Allan Poe in Baltimore is widely believed; there are even persons who, stopping off in Baltimore to eat oysters, go to look at it. As a matter of fact, no such monument exists. All that the explorer actually finds is a cheap and hideous tombstone in the corner of a Presbyterian churchyard—a tombstone quite as bad as the worst in Père La Chaise. For twenty-six years after Poe's death there was not even this: the grave remained wholly unmarked. Poe had surviving relatives in Baltimore, and they were well-to-do. One day one of them ordered a local stonecutter to put a plain stone over the grave. The stonecutter hacked it out and was preparing to haul it to the churchyard when a runaway freight-train smashed into his stoneyard and broke the stone to bits. Thereafter the Poes seem to have forgotten Cousin Edgar; at all events, nothing further was done.

The existing tombstone was erected by a committee

of Baltimore schoolmarms, and cost about $1,000. It took the dear girls ten long years to raise the money. They started out with a "literary entertainment" which yielded $380. This was in 1865. Six years later the fund had made such slow progress that, with accumulated interest, it came to but $587.02. Three years more went by: it now reached $627.55. Then some anonymous Poeista came down with $100, two others gave $50 each, one of the devoted schoolmarms raised $52 in nickels and dimes, and George W. Childs agreed to pay any remaining deficit. During all this time not a single American author of position gave the project any aid. And when, finally, a stone was carved and set up and the time came for the unveiling, the only one who appeared at the ceremony was Walt Whitman. All the other persons present were Baltimore nobodies—chiefly schoolteachers and preachers. There were three set speeches—one by the principal of a local high school, the second by a teacher in the same seminary, and the third by a man who was invited to give his "personal recollections" of Poe, but who announced in his third sentence that "I never saw Poe but once, and our interview did not last an hour."

This was the gaudiest Poe celebration ever held in America. The poet has never enjoyed such august posthumous attentions as those which lately flattered the shade of James Russell Lowell. At his actual burial, in 1849, exactly eight persons were present, of whom six were relatives. He was planted, as I have said, in a Presbyterian churchyard, among generations of honest believers in infant damnation, but the officiating clergyman was a Methodist. Two days after his death a Baptist gentleman of God, the illustrious Rufus W. Griswold, printed a defamatory article upon him in the New York *Tribune*, and for years it set the tone of native criticism of him. And so he rests: thrust among Presbyterians by a Methodist and formally damned by a Baptist.

3

Memorial Service

Let us summon from the shades the immortal soul of James Harlan, born in 1820, entered into rest in 1899. In the year 1865 this Harlan resigned from the United States Senate to enter the cabinet of Abraham Lincoln as Secretary of the Interior. One of the clerks in that department, at $600 a year, was Walt Whitman, lately emerged from three years of hard service as an army nurse during the Civil War. One day, discovering that Whitman was the author of a book called "Leaves of Grass," Harlan ordered him incontinently kicked out, and it was done forthwith. Let us remember this event and this man; he is too precious to die. Let us repair, once a year,

to our accustomed houses of worship and there give
thanks to God that one day in 1865 brought together
the greatest poet that America has ever produced and
the damndest ass.

THE END

INDEX

Printed in the United States
17458LVS00002B/262-264